Sugarlicious

Sugarlicious

50 CUTE AND CLEVER TREATS
FOR EVERY OCCASION

Meaghan Mountford

HARLEQUIN®
www.Harlequin.com

SUGARLICIOUS

ISBN-13: 978-0-373-89254-9

Library of Congress Cataloging-in-Publication Data
Mountford, Meaghan, 1972-
Sugarlicious : 50 cute and clever treats for every occasion / Meaghan Mountford.
p. cm.
Includes index.
ISBN 978-0-373-89254-9
1. Cake decorating. 2. Sugar art. 3. Garnishes (Cooking) 4. Cookies. I. Title.
TX771.2.M68 2012
641.86'539--dc23   2011024149

www.Harlequin.com

Printed in U.S.A.

Design: Alissa Faden
Photography: Abby Greenawalt
Styling: Lisa Sikorski

For Greg and Maeve

CONTENTS

Preface

Welcome to *Sugarlicious*, where you can bake, craft and eat all in one place. Decorated cookies, cakes, cupcakes, cake pops, marshmallows and other sweets claim more and more space in the do-it-yourself world. And with more and more resources available to make unique, quirky treats, the possibilities can be overwhelming. Where do you start? Here. Within these pages, whether we're coating marshmallow pops in sprinkles or crafting a garden gnome to display on a cake, edible art is simplified, explained and moved within your creative reach. Imagine walking down the baking aisle at the craft store and feeling completely in control, full of knowledge and inspired by the products, rather than confused by all the tubs of fondant and tubes of food coloring.

This book is about creating cute and clever edible art. And if you're like me, when you see something cute and clever that you can also eat, you immediately wonder if you could make it yourself. I'm here to tell you that you can.

While I worked as a cookie decorator for almost a decade, only in the past few years have I moved beyond piping icing to delve into fondant, cupcakes, cakes, marshmallows, petits fours and candy clay. I've created hundreds of crafty sweets to share on my blog, *the decorated cookie.* And as the Edible Crafts editor of CraftGossip.com, I mine the internet daily for inspiration and information from the world of food crafts. Here I share what I've learned with you. Whether the world of decorating sweets intimidates you, intrigues you or consumes you, you are in the right place.

Farm Animal Snack Cakes, a Marshmallow Village, Candy Clay Critters, Solar System Cookie Pops, Milk Shake Cake Pops, Totally Edible Birthday Cake, Crazy Chocolate Lollipops—this is just a sampling of what you'll find inside. The crafts range from super easy to a little more challenging, and they may take anywhere from mere minutes to up to a couple of afternoons to complete. You'll find sweets for every event, occasion, holiday and season, so you can craft all year long. And the best part about edible art is mixing creativity with practicality. The desserts in this book are mixed, baked and crafted as works of art, but they are also meant to be given, served and eaten.

You'll find recipes for cookies, cupcakes, cakes, petits fours, icing, frosting, fondant, candy clay and more. You'll make cookie, marshmallow and cake pops. You'll learn how to mix frosting colors, pipe and flood icing, make fondant decorations, paint and stamp with food colors, use food coloring pens, work with edible icing sheets, decorate with sprinkles and candy, and so many other sweet techniques. With each project in *Sugarlicious*, you'll learn lasting skills that you can apply to the sweet canvas of your choice.

How to use this book

I suggest first skimming through the book just to get an idea of the many edible crafting possibilities. Then choose a treat you'd like to make from Part Three: The Crafts. Each craft has a list of the recipes and supplies you need, as well as the techniques you will use. Part One contains all the supplies used in the book, Part Two has all the recipes, and every technique is covered in Part Four. Gather everything you need, and dig in.

The difficulty of each craft is indicated by measuring cup icons. One cup signifies that the craft is easy, two cups indicate that it is moderately challenging and may take a bit more time, and three cups mean it is challenging. Beginners may want to start with a "one cup" craft, but even the most challenging crafts are absolutely doable for novices and experts alike. Most of the crafts in this book fall in the "two cup" category.

easy

moderate

challenging

If you are creating sweets for an event or a party, or to give as a gift, visit Part Five: The Wrapping, where you'll find packaging and serving ideas, including how to wrap favors and make arrangements from sweets on sticks. Make sure not to skip Part Six: Resources and Templates, which includes templates to accompany some of the crafts, as well as a Resources list. Supplies are easily accessible and most are found in your local craft store and supermarket, but finding the *right* supplies can be the toughest part of edible crafting if you don't know where to look or what to buy. Between the Supplies list in Part One and the Resources list in Part Six, you'll know exactly what to buy and where to get it.

Look out for Tips, Shortcuts and Ideas. These handy comments offer important time-saving solutions, suggestions to avoid mishaps, and ideas on how to mix and match the crafts.

tips

- Carefully read all the recipes and instructions in advance so you have the ingredients and supplies you need.

- Warning: Most crafts need to dry overnight! And many need to dry overnight between steps. So allow enough time if you are using the crafts for an event or giving them as a gift.

- Heed the "Shortcut" tips. If you are new to edible crafting, substituting store-bought ingredients is a great way to make crafting even easier.

- Creativity is encouraged! Once you learn the techniques, you'll be best able to make use of the "Ideas" offered for mixing and matching the sweets and the decorations.

PART ONE

The Supplies

This section covers everything you'll need to make the edible crafts in this book and beyond. You'll find a list of the supplies for baking and decorating, as well as suggestions for store-bought shortcuts. Each craft may require only a few of the supplies described below, but this comprehensive list of ingredients and equipment will serve as a useful reference throughout the book (a number of these are shown in the photos throughout this section and are indicated by a number following the description). For more tips on where to buy ingredients and supplies, check the Resources in Part Six.

recipe ingredients

Almost every recipe ingredient should be available in your supermarket. The exceptions—meringue powder, candy melts and glycerin—should be available in the baking aisle of any craft store. Check the Resources for stores and online suppliers.

BAKING SODA AND BAKING POWDER. Both are leavening agents, and baking powder contains baking soda, but even so, don't mix these up.

BUTTER. Use good-quality, unsalted sticks of butter. But if you accidentally bought salted, you'll be fine. Just reduce the salt in the recipe a smidgen.

CAKE FLOUR. The recipe for petits fours calls for cake flour. Cake flour has a lower protein content than all-purpose flour, which means it produces less gluten and makes for a smoother, more tender cake.

CANDY MELTS. These are also known as candy coating, wafers or confectionary coating. Of a similar consistency to chocolate chips and shaped like a disk, candy melts melt smoothly to easily coat sweets. Candy melts come in a variety of flavors (chocolate, peanut butter, vanilla, butterscotch) and colors (white, brown, green, orange, pink, red, purple, black, yellow, blue and more). You'll likely find the Wilton brand in the craft store. Other brands, available in specialty stores and online, include CK Products, Make 'n Mold and Merckens. Check the Resources for tips on where to buy.

CHOCOLATE CHIPS. To melt chocolate, chips are the easiest. Semisweet and milk chocolate are used here.

CLEAR VANILLA EXTRACT. If it's not in your supermarket, find this in the craft store or specialty stores. This is handy when making fondant and icing as the color stays a purer white. You may use regular vanilla extract in recipes calling for clear vanilla extract, but you will need to add additional white food coloring if your decoration requires white fondant or icing.

CONFECTIONERS' SUGAR. Confectioners' sugar is also known as powdered or icing sugar. Choose the larger, two-pound bag, as you will use quite a bit of this. If you use organic sugar in recipes for icing or fondant, note that it is not bleached, so your icings will have a brown hue. Simply add additional white food coloring to brighten the icing or fondant.

EGGS. Crack open the large ones.

FLOUR. Unless otherwise noted, use all-purpose flour.

FRUIT PRESERVES. You may brush petits fours with fruit preserves between layers, or coat the tops and sides to enable fondant to adhere when covering petits fours.

GELATIN. Available in the supermarket, this is used to make homemade rolled fondant.

GLYCERIN. A sweet, clear, viscous liquid useful to prevent icing from drying out, this is used to make homemade rolled fondant. Find it in the craft store.

GRANULATED SUGAR. Standard table sugar will do.

LIGHT CORN SYRUP. This is an ingredient in royal icing, fondant and candy clay, but it also makes a great "glue" for edible crafting.

MARSHMALLOWS. The minis are used in a shortcut, homemade fondant recipe, and standard-size marshmallows are a crafting canvas.

MERINGUE POWDER. Powdered egg whites mixed with sugar and/or stabilizers, meringue powder makes royal icing much easier to prepare and to keep without refrigeration. You'll likely find the Wilton brand in the craft store. Other brands, such as Ateco or CK Products, are found in specialty cake decorating stores. Williams-Sonoma also carries a good meringue powder in their stores.

MILK. You may use whole, low-fat or soy milk. I opt for whole milk.

SALT. Standard table salt will do.

SHREDDED COCONUT. Tint coconut different colors and press it into frosting to add texture when decorating sweets.

UNSWEETENED COCOA POWDER. This is for chocolate cakes, cookies and petits fours. Unsweetened cocoa powder is found in the supermarket. Such brands as Hershey's and Nestlé are readily available. Dutch-processed, or alkalized unsweetened cocoa powder, goes through a process to neutralize the acidity. You will find Dutch-processed cocoa, such as the Ghirardelli brand, in the supermarket or in upscale grocery stores. Dutch-processed cocoa does not react to baking soda, so this cocoa is usually used in recipes with baking powder. I tested both Dutch-processed and unsweetened cocoa powder in all the recipes here, and you may interchange the two, but I recommend the Dutch-processed for the petits fours recipe.

VANILLA, ALMOND AND OTHER FLAVORED EXTRACTS. Vanilla extract is a must. The other flavors are optional and can be added to sugar cookie dough. Almond, orange and raspberry work well. I use the real stuff, not imitation.

VEGETABLE SHORTENING. Crisco is my brand of choice.

supplies

For Baking

Baking supplies are found in supermarkets, department stores and craft stores.

BAKING TRAYS AND JELLY-ROLL PANS. Good-quality, sturdy trays and pans are a must. Insulated sheets are great for baking cookies, though you may also use jelly-roll pans (baking sheets with a one-inch wall around the edges). (1)

CAKE PANS. You should have round, metal cake pans and a glass or metal sheet-cake pan. The same rules above apply here. Use good-quality, sturdy pans. Dark or nonstick metal pans may require you to reduce the baking temperature by twenty-five degrees and to add a couple of minutes of baking time to prevent burning. For the crafts in this book you will need at least two nine-inch round cake pans for cakes and a nine-by-thirteen-inch sheet-cake pan for cake pops. I also have four six-inch round pans for smaller round cakes, which will also work for any cake craft in this book. (1)

COOKIE AND FONDANT CUTTERS. While I could write a treatise on the shapes and sizes of cookie cutters in the world, most of the cookie and fondant cutters used in this book are easy-to-find, basic shapes: circles, ovals, hearts, squares, flowers and leaves. Fondant cutters, which look like cookie cutters, only smaller, can also be used for mini cookies. Because we use a variety of sizes and basic shapes, I highly recommend purchasing sets. Leaf fondant cutters come in sets with one-, two- and three-inch cutters. Popular circle sizes include ½-inch, 1¼-inch, 2¼-inch, 2½-inch, 3-inch and larger. Squares are usually ½-inch, 1½-inch, 2¼-inch and larger. You should find these cutters at the craft store, but check the Resources for good online cookie-cutter shops.

tip

If you can't find the exact size circle or square fondant or cookie cutter required for a craft, you may usually substitute any circle or square that's about the same size. So, for example, if you can't find a 2¼-inch circle, just use a 2½-inch circle and adjust any decorating as needed. You can also use cookie and fondant cutters interchangeably as long as they are about the right size.

COOKIE STICKS. You must insert sticks in the cookies before baking to make cookie pops. While I (unofficially) use lollipop sticks in the oven to make cookie pops, because I prefer the smaller diameter, given the plastic coating on lollipop sticks, cookie sticks are recommended. Wilton makes cookie sticks, available in craft stores, in both the six-inch and eight-inch size. (10)

CUPCAKE LINERS AND BAKING CUPS. Choose any size (standard or mini) and color you desire. Note that when baked, the cake batter will show through most liners. You may want to double up the cupcake liners for a cleaner look, especially if using printed or specialized liners, so be sure to purchase enough. Find liners in the super-market or craft store, or check the Resources for tips on finding unique, themed liners. (7)

CUPCAKE TINS. Use good-quality, sturdy cup-cake or muffin tins. Standard muffin tins hold four ounces of batter in each cup; minis hold two ounces. I suggest paper cupcake liners or baking cups for all the cupcake crafts in this book. (1)

DOUGH SCRAPER. Also known as a bench scraper, this tool doubles as a cookie cutter for cutting long, straight sides. You can also use this to smooth frosting on a cake. (9)

LOLLIPOP STICKS. Use these for cookie, marshmallow, candy clay and cake pops. Find them in the craft store in four-, six-, eight- and twelve-inch sizes. Choose any desired size, though I tend to stick with the six-inch ones for most crafts. (10)

MEASURING CUPS AND SPOONS. You should have at least one set of measuring spoons and cups to measure dry ingredients and glass measuring cups for liquid measuring. This is nonnegotiable. (5)

METAL BOWL. Melt chocolate and candy melts in a metal bowl set over a saucepan of simmer-ing water if you don't own a double boiler.

MICROWAVE-SAFE BOWLS. You may also melt chocolate and candy melts in the micro-wave. Deep bowls are best for dipping sweets. I prefer microwave-safe plastic or silicone bowls for melting chocolate and candy melts, as they resist heat better. Overheating chocolate and candy melts makes a mess.

MIXING BOWLS. An assortment of sizes is helpful. (6)

PARCHMENT PAPER. A pantry staple, use this to line baking trays for no-stick cookies. Find it in the supermarket. Don't substitute wax paper, which will melt in the oven. (12)

PLASTIC CONTAINERS. Airtight containers with lids are perfect for storing unused royal icing, which will keep at room temperature for several weeks.

POPSICLE STICKS. Popsicle sticks are avail-able in the craft store, either in the baking aisle or the kids section. We use these only once in this book, to make Popsicle Cookie Pops. But you may use these for any pop in lieu of lollipop or cookie sticks, as long as they fit securely in the sweet. (11)

ROLLING PIN. Any standard, non-tapered roll-ing pin—wood, marble, silicone—will work to roll out cookie dough, fondant and candy clay. I pre-fer a standard wood rolling pin for cookies and a small silicone rolling pin to roll out fondant, but then I like to have extraneous kitchenware. (2)

ROLLING PIN GUIDE RINGS. These aren't essential, but they are extremely useful, espe-cially as I give you specific thickness measures to roll out fondant and cookie dough. Place these bands at the edges of your rolling pin to help you roll perfectly even fondant and cookie dough in ⅛-inch, ¼-inch and ⅜-inch thicknesses. Find them in craft stores, at specialty chain stores or online. (8)

SEALABLE BAGS. I keep my refrigerated cookie dough in ziplock bags, and you will use these to crush candy and tint coconut.

SILICONE BAKING MATS (OPTIONAL). You may use baking mats, such as SILPAT, to prevent sticking. But because parchment paper has so many other uses, I use it to line my cookie sheets instead of baking mats.

SPATULAS. At least one flexible spatula is handy for scraping the sides of bowls. (3)

STANDING MIXER OR HANDHELD MIXER. If you use a standing mixer, use the flat beater for dough and the wire whip for icings. For those who prefer a more intimate mixing experience, a handheld electric mixer will work, too.

WAX PAPER. Use this to cover surfaces for easy cleanup. You'll also need wax paper when making candy clay and fondant decorations. (13)

WHISK. A whisk is necessary for sifting flour and other dry ingredients. (4)

WIRE RACKS. While I'm a renegade who lets her cookies cool on their trays, you will need cooling racks to coat sweets with poured sugar icing and to cool cakes. (1)

For Decorating

Most decorating supplies are found in the baking aisle of the craft store. Some supplies, like Soft Gel Paste food coloring, food coloring pens, and a greater variety of sprinkles and candies can be found online or in specialty cake decorating shops. Check the Resources for more information.

ASSORTED CANDIES AND SPRINKLES. These are a quick and easy decorating tool. You can use gumdrops, licorice lace, fruit leather, fruit chews, marshmallows, sparkling sugar, dragées, sprinkles and more. Sprinkles alone give you plenty of options. Just a sampling might include sanding and sparkling sugars, coarse sprinkles, edible glitter and "quins," which are the flat, shaped sprinkles, such as "confetti" sprinkles (also called polka dots), hearts, flowers, leaves and more. Check out "How to Use Sprinkles and Candy" in the Techniques section for more information and the Resources section for tips on where to buy these products. (34)

CAKE BOARDS. These cardboard rounds or rectangles, available in the craft store, are handy to rest cakes on, especially when traveling. (27)

CAKE STAND. A cake stand is useful not only for displaying your cake, but also to raise your cake for easier frosting. I just turn the cake on the cake stand, but you can also use a turntable.

CHOCOLATE WAFER COOKIES. Store-bought chocolate wafer cookies, when crushed, can be used as "dirt" on chocolate icing. (35)

COUPLERS. Couplers are cylinders that fit inside decorating bags with rings that screw on the end to hold on decorating tips. Couplers allow you to easily change decorating tips. Choose the standard size. The Wilton brand, which I use, is found in most craft stores. Have plenty of these available. (16)

DECORATING TIPS. Metal decorating tips control the flow of icing from a decorating bag. The larger numbers have larger openings. Tips are primarily divided between round tips (a simple round opening) and textured tips (with teeth or ridges at the opening). For cookie decorating and piping royal icing, you will use only round tips numbered 2, 3, 4 and 5. For frosting cupcakes, you may use a large round tip, numbered 10, 11 or 12. Or, frost cupcakes with open star tips, a type of textured tip that forms decorative ridges in your icing. I prefer open star tips numbered 20, 21, 22, 32 and 199. You'll also find plenty of options to pipe buttercream frosting with textured tips to make stars, flowers, leaves, ruffles, basket weaves and more. We do this infrequently in this book, but we do use a closed star tip, size 30, for the Hyacinth Cookie Pops, and the multi-opening tip, size 233, to make "grass" on the Sporty Petits Fours. Wilton is my preferred brand. Ateco also makes quality decorating tips, available in specialty stores or online (check the Resources). Decorating tips are inexpensive and very useful, so I have quite a few of each size. Make sure to buy the standard decorating tips that fit the standard couplers, not the huge ones. (15)

DISPOSABLE DECORATING BAGS. Necessary for piping royal icing and frosting, even melted chocolate and candy melts, these are a pantry staple. I use the twelve-inch, clear, plastic, disposable decorating bags. Find them in the craft store, along with couplers and decorating tips. Again, Wilton is my preferred brand. They do come in larger sizes, too, which is useful when piping frosting on a lot of cupcakes. (18)

DRINK CHARMS, CUPCAKE TOPPERS AND PICKS. Little plastic charms, cupcake picks and cupcake toppers, available from party stores or baking supply stores, are fun decorating tools. Be sure to warn guests that these are not edible, and avoid or take particular care giving treats with inedible decorations to children! (37)

EDIBLE ICING SHEETS. These are letter-size sheets of paper with strips or cupcake-size circles with edible "stickers" in a variety of designs. Simply cut to shape (if using the strips), peel and stick on prepared icing. Find tips on where to buy these in the Resources section. (38)

EDIBLE WRITERS. Also known as food coloring pens, food coloring markers, food decorator pens and gourmet writers, these look exactly like conventional markers but contain edible ink. Do not confuse these with the candy writers or icing writers in tubes from the craft store, which I find too cumbersome to use. You may find some edible writers in craft stores, likely the Wilton FoodWriter, though your color choices are limited there and the FoodWriters have thick tips, which are more difficult to use for fine detail. I recommend, in this order, the set of ten AmeriColor Gourmet Writer Food Decorator pens, the ten-pack fine-line Food Coloring Marker set from FooDoodler, and the Kopykake Coloring Pens, a set of ten. Check the Resources for where to buy these. (42)

FONDANT SMOOTHER. Use this paddle to smooth fondant when covering cakes. (22)

FUNNEL. I use a lot of sprinkles. Funnels help when pouring excess sprinkles back in their containers. (28)

GEL PASTE FOOD COLORING. Gel pastes are the best for edible crafting. The concentrated gel pastes available in craft stores, most often the Wilton brand, come in a variety of colors, work well and are accessible. But I find they have a bitter, metallic taste. I use Soft Gel Paste food coloring by AmeriColor, which is available online or in specialty cake decorating stores. They blend well, come in every color imaginable and are tasteless. Ateco also makes a good brand, Spectrum. Check the Resources for tips on where to buy these food-coloring products.

A little goes a long way, so you should be fine with the smaller, .75-ounce sizes. The larger bottles, 4.5 ounces, are useful, however, when you have hundreds of cookies or cakes to decorate, or for colors that you will use often and in larger quantities, such as white and black. (14)

MALLET. Place hard candy or chocolate cookies in sealed bags and crush with a mallet. You may also use a rolling pin in lieu of a mallet. (31)

OFFSET SPATULAS. I find these essential for frosting cupcakes and cakes. I have a small one for cupcakes and a large one for cakes. (32)

OIL-BASED FOOD COLORING. This food coloring is also called candy color. Wilton, AmeriColor and Chefmaster all offer oil-based food coloring. Find the Wilton brand in the craft store and other brands online or in specialty cake decorating stores. These are necessary when tinting candy melts, as you *cannot* add gel pastes to melted candy melts or chocolate. Because candy melts come in so many premixed colors, I add candy color sparingly. However, candy colors are very useful when working with candy clay (which is made with candy melts or chocolate), because you can tint one batch of white candy clay many different colors. Oil-based food coloring comes in basic colors, including red, orange, yellow, green, blue, purple, black and pink, though you'll find a bit more variety with the Chefmaster and AmeriColor brands.

PAINTBRUSHES. You will use these for painting cookies and to brush on corn syrup to use as glue. You may also use these to paint lollipop sticks. Choose smaller-size brushes, both round and flat, and some very small detail brushes. Find these in the fine arts section of the craft store. (40)

PALETTES. No need to buy special palettes. Use a clean plastic egg carton, a paper plate or even a piece of wax paper as a palette for food coloring "paint." (39)

PAPER TOWELS. I use a lot of paper towels. A lot. Always keep paper towels handy when crafting.

PASTRY BRUSH. Brush cakes or large areas of sweets with corn syrup using a pastry brush to attach fondant or sprinkles. (20)

PIZZA CUTTER. A sharp knife or dough scraper works, too, but a pizza cutter is a great tool for cutting strips of rolled-out fondant. (23)

PLASTIC GLOVES. I personally don't use these and walk around with stained hands, but kneading food coloring into fondant and candy clay will stain your hands, so you may opt to wear gloves.

PRETZEL STICKS. Pretzel sticks make good stems for pumpkins and apples. (33)

RUBBER BANDS. No need to buy fancy rings, as rubber bands close decorating bags tightly so icing and frosting don't ooze out the top when you are piping. (17)

RUBBER STAMPS. Rubber stamps are a quick and easy decorating tool. Find them in the scrapbooking section of the craft store, or check the Resources for online shops. Clear stamps are too smooth for the coloring to stick, so make sure to choose rubber stamps. (41)

SCISSORS. Scissors will come in handy throughout, but they are essential for snipping the tips from decorating bags. (30)

SERRATED KNIFE. Use this for de-crumbing and leveling cakes or to shorten the ice cream cones for the Winter Wonderland Cake. (19)

SMALL KNIVES. These are great for cutting cookie dough shapes and fondant shapes, and for scraping mistakes. I use a sharp paring knife. (24, 25)

STYROFOAM BLOCKS. These are found in the craft store. You will need these to prop up cake pops and other sweets on a stick to dry. You will also use Styrofoam blocks to make arrangements with sweets on a stick. (29)

TAPE MEASURE OR RULER. You'll be surprised how often you reach for a ruler. Measuring keeps things precise. You'll need a measuring tool for decorative marshmallow pops and to cover cakes with fondant. (21)

TOOTHPICKS. Another pantry staple, use these for testing cakes and cupcakes, for mixing food coloring into icing, for unclogging decorating tips and for encouraging icing when using the flooding cookie-decorating technique. (26)

TWEEZERS. I stick with careful fingers, but you may use tweezers to add sprinkles and dragées.

WHOLE CLOVES. Cloves make good stems, as well as good arms for snowmen. Just be sure to remove them before eating. (36)

Store-bought substitutions

Eliminate hours of prep time and get to the fun part, decorating, more quickly by using store-bought substitutions.

BROWNIES. Store-bought brownies also make a good substitute for the homemade cake in petits fours, especially for the Sporty Petits Fours craft.

CAKE AND COOKIE MIXES. Any mix will work for cakes, cupcakes and cookies, but when using store-bought sugar cookie mix to make cutout decorated cookies, be sure to follow the recipe on the box for "rolled" cookies not "drop" cookies.

FONDANT. Fondant is the most important store-bought substitution in this book. A one-and-a-half-pound or five-pound box of ready-made bright white fondant from the craft store or specialty cake supply store saves much aggravation. The craft store will likely carry the Wilton brand. If you are making your sweets for an event, I suggest upgrading to a brand such as Satin Ice, in a two- or five-pound tub (available online or in specialty stores) or Duff's two-pound tub (available in Michaels craft store or online). You can also purchase fondant in a variety of colors. Satin Ice offers the best array of colors, followed by the Duff brand. Check the Resources for tips on where to buy these products. Unless you are covering a cake or a lot of treats, I buy white fondant and tint it with my own colors.

FROSTING. While there is no substitute for homemade royal icing, which dries hard so you can package sweets, you can substitute store-bought cans of frosting when a project calls for buttercream frosting.

MARSHMALLOWS. With store-bought marshmallows and a food coloring pen, you can create edible art in less than five minutes.

POUND CAKE. Also substitute store-bought, frozen pound cake for the homemade cake in petits fours.

SNACK CAKES. Oreo Cakesters, Little Debbie snack cakes, Tastykakes and Hostess products make good substitutes for the homemade petits fours. I highly recommend the Oreo Cakesters.

For Packaging (optional)

All these supplies are optional, but below are some things you may need to package, wrap, give or serve your sweets. Most of the items can be found in any major craft store, but you'll find more information on where to buy specialty items in the Resources section.

CELLOPHANE. Wrap plates of sweets with sheets of cellophane.

CELLOPHANE BAGS. Small (about four inches wide by six inches long) or larger (about four by nine inches) cellophane favor bags are the perfect solution for packaging cookies on or off a stick, cake pops, marshmallows and marshmallow pops or petits fours. Tie them closed with ribbon. Find them in the craft store or online.

CIRCLE PUNCH. Make tags instantly with a circle or other shaped punch.

DECORATIVE PAPER. Preprinted paper is great for paper cones and other do-it-yourself packaging. Find this in the scrapbooking section of the craft store, or check the Resources for tips on where to buy this product.

DOUBLE-SIDED TAPE. It is handy when assembling paper embellishments and packaging as the tape is hidden.

FABRIC. Package sweets in fabric sacks, or use fabric to top mason jars.

GIFT BOXES. Pack edible gifts in bakery boxes. Check the Resources for where to buy these boxes.

HOLE PUNCH. Use this for tags and labels. It is especially handy when adding tags to lollipop sticks.

JARS. I love mason jars as a packaging idea for small sweets. Just add labels and ribbon. Find mason jars in the craft store, supermarket or hardware store.

KEEPSAKE CONTAINERS. Choose large, shallow, open containers and baskets to make arrangements of sweets on sticks.

PAPER AND CARD STOCK. Use paper with a weight and stiffness to it, such as photo paper, or a card stock, to make tags and labels. Letter-size paper is ideal for easy printing.

PAPER TRIMMER. An inexpensive paper trimmer from the craft store saves much cutting time and is great for slicing long, straight lines.

RIBBON AND BAKERY TWINE. With the nearly infinite options out there, you can easily dress up any edible gift.

SCISSORS. You can't get by without these.

STYROFOAM BLOCKS. Found in the craft store, these are used to make arrangements of sweets on sticks. Find a block that fits securely in your chosen container, or simply wrap a block of Styrofoam with tissue paper or decorative paper.

TAGS. Store-bought tags are just as useful as homemade, and quicker.

TISSUE PAPER. Use tissue paper around the base of your arrangements or for wrapping. But just be sure not to put tissue paper directly against a sweet, or the oils will mark the paper.

PART TWO

The Recipes

This section includes basic recipes for the sweets decorated in this book: cookies, cakes, cupcakes, cake pops, petits fours, icings, frostings, fondant and candy clay. Feel free to substitute your own favorite recipes; and you'll find plenty of suggestions for substituting store-bought mixes or products, too.

cookies

You can use your favorite recipe for rolled cookies, or even store-bought mixes, but these cookie recipes have been well tested to work for the crafts here. They hold their shape and can be baked thickly to accommodate sticks for cookie pops. You may interchange the sugar cookie, flavored sugar cookie or chocolate cookie recipes in any craft that uses cookies, unless otherwise noted.

Sugar Cookies

1 cup (2 sticks) unsalted butter, slightly softened
1 cup confectioners' sugar
1 egg
1 teaspoon vanilla extract
2½ cups all-purpose flour
½ teaspoon salt

1. In the bowl of a standing mixer with a flat beater or in a large bowl with an electric hand mixer, combine butter and sugar at low speed. Switch to medium speed and blend well. Blend in the egg. Add vanilla extract and blend, scraping down sides of bowl as needed. Briefly whisk together flour and salt in a separate large bowl and gradually blend into the wet ingredients.

2. Cover dough with plastic wrap or place in a sealable plastic bag, and chill in the refrigerator for 2 hours. Follow the instructions on page (23) for rolling, cutting and baking cookies.

3. Preheat oven to 375 degrees F. Bake for about 12 to 16 minutes or until edges are golden brown. Reduce baking time for mini cookies (1 to 2 inches across) by a few minutes. Add several minutes of baking time for larger cookies or for cookies on a stick, which are thicker. Because cookie size varies in this book, be vigilant when your cookies are in the oven and watch for browned edges, as that is the best way to determine if cookies are done.

Yield: 25 to 30 medium-size cookies (2 to 4 inches across), 65 to 70 mini cookies (1 to 2 inches across). Note that cookies on a stick, which are rolled more thickly, may yield fewer cookies.

Flavored Sugar Cookies

Prepare the recipe above, but add 1½ teaspoons almond extract with the vanilla extract. You may also try orange, raspberry or other flavored extracts in lieu of the almond extract.

tips

It's important in cookie decorating that cookies keep their shape when baking, especially when making cookies with holes, such as ornament cookies, and for cookie pops. Here are some tips to avoid spreading:

• Use good-quality, sturdy baking trays or insulated cookie sheets lined with parchment paper. No flimsy trays, please!

• Make sure your oven is fully preheated, and make sure your oven temperature is accurate with an oven thermometer.

• Chill your cookie dough well before rolling it out. It should be pliable but not at all mushy. You may also chill a baking tray with your cutout shapes in the refrigerator for fifteen minutes before baking.

make-ahead tips

- You can make cookie dough up to three days in advance if it is kept in a sealed bag or container in the refrigerator. When ready to use, let the dough sit at room temperature for thirty minutes to an hour, or until pliable but still chilled. You may also freeze unbaked dough. Keep the dough in a sealed, freezer-safe bag. When needed, remove it from the freezer and let it thaw fully in the sealed bag in the fridge, then leave it at room temperature until pliable.

- You may cut out and bake cookies and keep them at room temperature, either undecorated or decorated, up to a week.

- To freeze cookies that are cut out and baked, but not decorated, stack them carefully and wrap in freezer-safe, sealed bags. Place them in a sturdy box or container to prevent freezer accidents. Let them thaw at room temperature *fully* in the sealed bags before removing them.

- To freeze cutout, baked and decorated cookies, arrange them in a single layer in a gallon-size, freezer-safe, sealed plastic bag (you might only fit four to eight cookies per bag). Stack the bags of cookies in a box or container and freeze. Thaw them at room temperature *fully* before removing them from the sealed bags. Do not remove the cookies from the sealed bags before they are thawed, or the icing may bleed.

Chocolate Cookies

1 cup (2 sticks) unsalted butter, slightly softened
1 cup granulated sugar
1 egg
1 teaspoon vanilla extract
2 cups all-purpose flour
½ cup unsweetened cocoa powder
½ teaspoon baking soda
½ teaspoon salt

1. In the bowl of a standing mixer with a flat beater or in a large bowl with an electric hand mixer, blend butter and sugar at medium speed. Add the egg and vanilla extract and blend, scraping down sides of bowl as needed. Mix flour, cocoa, baking soda and salt in a separate large bowl with a whisk, and gradually add to the wet ingredients until blended.

2. Cover dough with plastic wrap or place in a sealable plastic bag, and chill in the refrigerator for 2 hours. Follow the instructions for rolling, cutting and baking cookies.

3. Preheat oven to 375 degrees F. Bake for 12 to 16 minutes or until edges are crisp. Mini cookies (1 to 2 inches across) will take less time. Larger cookies or cookies on a stick, which are thicker, will take a few extra minutes. Because cookie size varies in this book, be vigilant when your cookies are in the oven and watch for browned edges, as that is the best way to determine if cookies are done.

Yield: 25 to 30 medium-size cookies (2 to 4 inches), 65 to 70 mini cookies (1 to 2 inches). Note that cookies on a stick, which are rolled more thickly, may yield fewer cookies.

Rolling, cutting and baking cookies.

Start with nicely chilled dough that is still pliable. If your dough is overchilled and too hard, let it sit at room temperature until pliable, about half an hour or more. On a lightly floured surface with floured hands, briefly knead one-third of your batch of chilled cookie dough into a ball. Flatten the ball a bit with your palm, and roll dough ¼ inch thick. If you are making cookies on a stick, you will need to roll out the dough so it is about ⅜ inch thick, and if making ornaments, ⅛ inch thick. If desired, place rolling pin rings at either end of the rolling pin to help you roll perfectly even dough. You should have a smooth circle of dough. If the dough has cracks, briefly knead the dough and roll again.

Use a cookie cutter, fondant cutter, knife or dough scraper to cut your shapes as closely to each other as possible to minimize handling. If you are using a template instead of a cookie cutter, cut out your shape from a piece of paper or card stock, place on top of the rolled-out dough and cut around the edges with a sharp knife. Smooth the edges with your fingers. Place cookies one inch apart on a baking tray lined with parchment paper and bake in a fully preheated oven. Cookies are done when edges are golden. For the sake of stability, let cookies on a stick bake an extra couple of minutes to ensure the insides aren't soft.

Cookies on a stick.

When choosing cookies to put on a stick, it's best to use small cutters—a maximum of three to four inches across—as larger cookies decrease stability. I usually use a six-inch stick for cookie pops, but if you are making a cookie arrangement in a container, you might want to use a variety of sizes. While I've always used lollipop sticks for cookie pops, as I prefer the smaller diameter, cookie sticks, which are free of plastic coating, are recommended.

Follow the recipes for sugar, flavored or chocolate rolled cookies. After chilling, roll out dough thickly enough to accommodate the stick, about ⅜ inch. Gently insert the stick into the bottom of the cookie shape, centered in the cookie's thickness, and press about halfway into the cookie. Pat dough back in place if necessary. The stick should fit fully in the cookie. No stick should be showing on the top or bottom of the cookie. Arrange on your baking tray lined with parchment paper. Make sure none of the cookies or sticks touch each other on the baking tray. Bake cookies according to the recipe, allowing a couple extra minutes of baking time to ensure the cookie centers are baked, and let cool completely before decorating.

cakes, cupcakes and cake pops

You can use any of your favorite cake recipes, but I've provided recipes for classic yellow cake and chocolate cake. Use these recipes or store-bought cake mix to make round layer cakes, cupcakes and sheet cakes for cake pops. You may also make mini cupcakes from the recipes. Just adjust your decorating to make everything smaller. Unless otherwise noted, you may interchange the yellow or chocolate cake recipes in any craft that calls for cakes, cupcakes or cake pops.

Yellow Cake and Cupcakes

2¾ cups all-purpose flour

2½ teaspoons baking powder

¼ teaspoon salt

1 cup (2 sticks) unsalted butter, slightly softened

2 cups granulated sugar

4 eggs

1½ teaspoons vanilla extract

1 cup milk

1. Preheat oven to 350 degrees F. Grease and flour cake pans or line cupcake tins with baking cups.

2. In a large bowl, combine flour, baking powder and salt and whisk together. In the bowl of a standing mixer with the flat beater, or with a handheld electric mixer, cream butter and sugar together until well blended.

3. Add the eggs, one at a time, blending well after each addition. Add the vanilla extract and blend. Alternating, add the milk and flour mixture to the butter and sugar mixture, blending well with each addition, scraping down the sides of the bowl with a spatula as needed.

shortcut

This is one place where I often save time by going straight for the store-bought cake mix. Store-bought cake mix with a homemade buttercream frosting is the perfect combination of time-saving yumminess.

4. Pour the batter evenly in prepared pans or cupcake tins. Bake 20 to 25 minutes for standard cupcakes, 12 to 15 minutes for mini cupcakes, 30 to 35 minutes for a round cake, 35 to 45 minutes for a sheet cake, or until a toothpick inserted in the center comes out clean and the edges start to brown.

5. For a round layer cake, when the cake is cool enough to touch, turn out on wire racks to cool completely. For cupcakes, remove from the cupcake tins when cool enough to touch.

Yield: Makes 1 nine-inch cake (2 layers), 1 sheet cake, 24 cupcakes, 48 mini cupcakes or 60 cake pops. This recipe will also make 4 layers of a six-inch cake.

Chocolate Cake and Cupcakes

2½ cups all-purpose flour

1 cup unsweetened cocoa powder

2 teaspoons baking powder

½ teaspoon salt

1 cup butter, softened

2 cups sugar

3 eggs

1 teaspoon vanilla extract

1½ cups milk

1. Preheat oven to 350 degrees F. Grease and flour cake pans or line cupcake tins with baking cups. In a large bowl, briefly whisk together the dry ingredients and set aside.

2. In a standing mixer with a flat beater or with a handheld electric mixer, cream the butter on medium speed. Add the sugar and blend well. Add the eggs, one at a time, beating well after each addition. Add the vanilla extract and blend. Gradually add the flour mixture to the sugar and butter mixture alternately with the milk until well blended, scraping down the sides of the bowl with a spatula as needed.

3. Pour the batter evenly in prepared pans or cupcake tins. Bake 20 to 25 minutes for standard cupcakes, 12 to 15 minutes for mini cupcakes, 30 to 35 minutes for a round cake, 35 to 45 minutes for a sheet cake, or until a toothpick inserted in the center comes out clean.

4. For a round layer cake, when the cake is cool enough to touch, turn out on wire racks to cool completely. For cupcakes, remove from the cupcake tins when cool enough to touch.

Yield: Makes 1 nine-inch cake (2 layers), 1 sheet cake, 24 cupcakes, 48 mini cupcakes or 60 cake pops. This recipe will also make 4 layers of a six-inch cake.

Cake pops. To make cake pops, bake a nine-by-thirteen-inch sheet cake using the recipes here, your favorite recipe, or a box of store-bought cake mix. Let the cake cool completely and crumble into a large bowl. Stir in 1⅓ cups of buttercream frosting (this is about half the recipe for buttercream frosting in this book) or use three-quarters of a container of store-bought frosting and mix well, pressing the cake and frosting together with the back of a spoon or, preferably, mixing them with your hands until you have a texture that is wet, smooth and able to be formed.

Between the palms of your hands, roll the mixture into balls 1½ inches in diameter and place them on a baking tray lined with wax paper. Freeze for fifteen minutes, no longer. Move the tray of cake balls to the refrigerator to keep them firm but not frozen. Work with a few cake balls at a time, while keeping the remainder in the fridge.

To make a cake pop, dip the tip of a lollipop stick in melted candy melts and insert gently in the cake ball. Then dip the cake pop in melted candy melts (see the Techniques section) and decorate as you desire.

> ### tip
>
> Store-bought cake mix will make about 48 cake pops; the recipe here will make about 60. You may divide your nine-by-thirteen-inch cake in half or quarters. Simply freeze the unused portions in freezer-safe, sealable bags, and adjust the frosting accordingly by a half or quarter (so use ⅓ cup frosting for a quarter of the cake and use ⅔ cup frosting for half a cake).

petits fours and little cakes

Traditional petits fours are made with an almond sponge cake, split, filled with jam and iced or glazed. The recipes here for petits fours and chocolate petits fours are a bit untraditional. But they are perfect for edible crafting, as they are dense, flavorful cakes ideal for cutting up, covering and decorating. Use the two recipes interchangeably in any craft that calls for petits fours, unless otherwise noted.

Petits Fours

4 tablespoons milk

4 eggs

2 teaspoons vanilla extract

2 cups cake flour

1 cup sugar

1 teaspoon baking powder

¼ teaspoon salt

1 cup (2 sticks) plus 2 tablespoons unsalted butter (18 tablespoons)

1. Preheat oven to 350 degrees F. Line a jelly-roll pan with parchment paper. Lightly grease the parchment paper. Set aside.

2. Combine the milk, eggs and vanilla extract in a medium bowl with a whisk, and set aside. In a large bowl, combine the dry ingredients with a whisk. In the bowl of a standing mixer fitted with a flat beater or in a large bowl with a handheld electric mixer, cream the butter. Gradually mix in half of the flour mixture. Add the wet mixture and blend well. Gradually mix in the remainder of the flour mixture, scraping down the sides of the bowl with a spatula as needed.

3. Pour the batter onto the prepared pan and spread evenly with a spatula to fill the pan. Bake for 25 to 30 minutes, or until a toothpick inserted in the center comes out clean.

   Yield: About 40 two-inch squares or circles, or 20 petits fours if stacked in 2 layers. Note

shortcut

Substitute homemade petits fours with a frozen pound cake or store-bought snack cakes such as Oreo Cakesters, Little Debbie snack cakes or Hostess snack cakes. I recommend Oreo Cakesters, as they are a perfect size, density and stickiness, so fondant adheres easily. Use a sharp knife, dough scraper or a cookie cutter to trim edges and make squares, or just keep the circle shape. However, I warn you to prepare your sweet tooth, as you will be adding icing and sweets on top of sugar-filled treats.

that some crafts may require larger or smaller squares or circles, which will affect your yield.

Chocolate Petits Fours

Add ½ cup cocoa powder, preferably Dutch-processed, or alkalized unsweetened cocoa powder, to the dry ingredients in the recipe.

Cutting and stacking petits fours.

To make square petits fours, use a sharp knife, a dough scraper or a square cookie cutter about 1½ inches wide and 2¼ inches long. For circles, use a circle cookie cutter with a diameter between 1½ inches and 2¼ inches.

The petits fours in these recipes are between ½ inch and ¾ inch thick. You may either use a single layer for your decorated treats or stack two layers for a taller cake. To stack, cut out shapes, and then spread a thin layer of butter-cream frosting (homemade or store-bought), fruit preserves or royal icing on a petit four and stack with a second layer.

Find tips on covering your petits fours with poured sugar icing or fondant in the Techniques section.

icing, frosting and fondant

Icing, frosting and fondant cause the most confusion and worry in the world of edible crafting, so the information below should clarify things. Fondant, which is used frequently for the crafts in this book, is especially daunting. But I promise it needn't be.

ROYAL ICING will be used primarily to decorate cookies in this book. Traditional royal icing is a white icing made from whipped egg whites and confectioners' sugar that dries very hard. But a bit too hard for my taste. The user-friendly recipe found here is made from meringue powder (a dried egg-white mixture), water and confectioners' sugar. The flavoring and shorten-

ing added to the recipe means the icing won't dry rock hard like traditional royal icing, but the yummy taste is well worth it, and the icing will dry hard enough to handle so you can package and even ship your decorated cookies.

Using meringue powder in place of real egg whites enables you to keep the icing stored at room temperature for several weeks. Because we will use the icing in the same way you would use a traditional royal icing, I still call it royal icing to distinguish it from the other icings.

POURED SUGAR ICING is a simple mixture of confectioners' sugar and milk. It serves as a substitute for royal icing when decorating cookies. Rather than pipe icing with a decorating bag to top cookies, you can pour this icing over the cookies and let it dry overnight to create a beautiful, smooth canvas for decorating. You may also coat petits fours with poured sugar icing, as is the petits fours tradition, though I prefer to cover them with fondant. Icing shows the cut cake's imperfections.

tips on royal icing

- You may halve this recipe, but I never do. This icing stores well in a sealed container at room temperature, and it's useful to have extra to allow for errors, especially when you are new to cookie decorating or trying out new designs.

- It is much easier to thin icing with a few drops of water later, when you are working with a finished batch, than it is to thicken with powdery, messy confectioners' sugar. If you are unsure if your frosting is too thick or too thin, play it safe and thicken it. Once you start working frequently with royal icing, you'll learn what consistency works best for you.

- A two-pound bag of confectioners' sugar has just under eight cups. A one-pound box has just under four cups. I always buy the two-pound bags. You can never have enough confectioners' sugar!

BUTTERCREAM FROSTING has a flavor that can't be beat. But this frosting, a mixture of butter, powdered sugar and milk, never dries fully, so it's not ideal for decorating cookies. You will use buttercream frosting to top cakes and cupcakes and in the cake pops recipe. You may also first spread buttercream frosting on cookies, petits fours, cakes or cupcakes that will be coated with fondant.

FONDANT is also known as "rolled fondant icing," not to be confused with poured fondant, which we don't use in this book. You might love it or fear it. I have mixed feelings toward the stuff, but I find it essential for edible crafting, as do most professional cake decorators. About half of the crafts in this book rely on fondant. Use fondant to top cookies, cakes, cupcakes and petits fours to make a perfect crafting canvas, or use fondant to make decorations. It is malleable and smooth, so it can be rolled out, cut out and manipulated, but it stiffens well enough to make dimensional designs. While many who've never worked with fondant are wary, fondant is surprisingly user-friendly and works wonderfully to give a finished look to your sweet. I promise you need not fear fondant.

Because homemade fondant doesn't taste significantly different from store-bought, I highly recommend purchasing store-bought, white, premade fondant (see the Supplies list in Part One and the Resources section in Part Six for tips on brands to buy and where to buy), but you will find recipes for fondant and a shortcut marshmallow fondant here.

Royal Icing

4 tablespoons meringue powder
½ cup cold water
6 to 8 cups confectioners' sugar
2 tablespoons vegetable shortening
2 tablespoons light corn syrup
1 teaspoon vanilla extract*

*You may use clear vanilla extract so your icing is closer to true white, but I usually add Bright White coloring, anyway, for a pure white, so I often stick with my regular extract.

1. In the bowl of a standing mixer with a wire whip or in a large bowl with an electric hand mixer, mix meringue powder and cold water for several seconds on low speed. Switch to the highest speed and whip for several minutes, until fluffy and stiff peaks form and the mixture looks like snow.

2. On low speed, mix in 3 cups of the confectioners' sugar until blended. Add shortening, corn syrup and vanilla extract and blend. Add 3 more cups of confectioners' sugar and blend on low. Check the consistency of the icing and, if needed, add 1 more cup of confectioners' sugar, and up to 2 more cups. Your brand of meringue powder, the humidity and other such factors affect consistency, but I almost always end up with about 7 cups of confectioners' sugar.

3. Your royal icing should not be so stiff that it's difficult to manage, but it shouldn't be so runny that it drizzles or loses its shape. Take a spoonful and turn it over. The icing should cling to the spoon. After several seconds, the icing may slowly fall into the bowl. To thicken royal icing, add ¼ cup confectioners' sugar at a time and blend well. To thin, add 1 teaspoon water at a time and blend well.

4. You will use royal icing to decorate cookies. For the flooding technique of cookie

decorating, you will need to thin this icing. You may also use royal icing to pipe designs on cake pops, petits fours or fondant-topped sweets.

Yield: 4 cups of icing, or 5 to 6 frosting bags.

Poured Sugar Icing

4 cups confectioners' sugar
¼ cup light corn syrup
¼ cup milk, plus additional
1 teaspoon clear vanilla extract*

*You may substitute regular vanilla extract, but note you will need to add additional white food coloring to make a bright white icing.

1. Mix all the ingredients in a large bowl with a whisk.

2. Continue to add milk (about 1 to 2 tablespoons additional) until the mixture is of a pouring consistency. The mixture should not be so thin that it drains off your sweet, leaving only a thin coat. But it shouldn't be so thick that it sits on top of the sweet. A good

way to check your consistency is the ten-second rule. Take a spoonful and drizzle over the bowl. The drizzled icing should take about ten seconds to fall into itself and disappear.

Use poured sugar icing to coat cookies. You may also coat petits fours or pound cake and snack cake substitutes with it, and this makes a tastier alternative to covering with fondant. However, poured sugar icing shows the imperfections on the cut sides of petits fours and cakes. Find tips on how to cover sweets with poured sugar icing in Part Four.

Yield: 1¾ cups of icing. Be prepared to make a second batch of poured sugar icing to decorate an entire batch of cookies or small cakes, but I find it's best to work with 1 batch at a time, as excess poured sugar icing doesn't keep as well as royal icing.

Buttercream Frosting

½ cup (1 stick) plus 2 tablespoons of unsalted butter, softened
4½ cups confectioners' sugar
3 to 6 tablespoons milk
1 teaspoon vanilla extract
pinch of salt (optional)

1. With a wire whip in the bowl of a standing mixer, or in a large bowl with a handheld electric mixer on medium speed, cream the butter. Add 3 cups of the confectioners' sugar, 1 cup at a time, blending well after each addition. The mixture may still be dry and crumbly.

2. Add 3 tablespoons of the milk and the vanilla extract and blend well. Blend in the remaining 1½ cups of confectioners' sugar. Blend in the salt, if using.

3. Add more milk to thin and more

tip

These buttercream frosting recipes are pretty forgiving. You can add more confectioners' sugar and milk to thicken or thin, respectively, without affecting the taste significantly. Since we primarily use this just to top cakes and cupcakes, not for decorating, nuances in the consistency are not as important as with royal icing, so you may use any consistency that works best for you. Go a bit thinner for easier spreading when frosting cakes and thicker when piping frosting on cupcakes so the frosting holds its shape.

confectioners' sugar to thicken as necessary to achieve desired consistency. The frosting should be thick enough to have stiff peaks when blended and to hold its shape when you scoop a spoonful, but it should be smooth enough to spread easily with a spatula.

Yield: 2¾ to 3 cups of frosting. Recipe may be halved.

Chocolate Buttercream Frosting

½ cup (1 stick) plus 2 tablespoons unsalted
    butter, softened
4½ cups confectioners' sugar
½ cup unsweetened cocoa powder
6 to 9 tablespoons milk
1 teaspoon vanilla extract
pinch of salt (optional)

1. With a wire whip in the bowl of a standing mixer, or in a large bowl with a handheld electric mixer on medium speed, cream the butter.

2. In a separate large bowl, mix confectioners' sugar and cocoa powder with a whisk. Add 1 cup of the dry mixture to the butter and blend. Add 3 tablespoons of the milk and the vanilla extract to the butter mixture and blend well.

3. Alternately add the remainder of the dry mixture and 3 more tablespoons of milk to the butter mixture. Add a pinch of salt to taste, if using. Add more milk, up to 3 tablespoons, until desired consistency is achieved. The frosting should be thick enough to have stiff peaks when blended and to hold its shape when you scoop a spoonful, but it should be smooth enough to spread easily with a spatula.

Yield: 2¾ to 3 cups of frosting. Recipe may be halved.

shortcut and tip

Homemade fondant doesn't taste significantly different from store-bought. Most bakeries purchase premade fondant. Rather than make your own, I recommend you buy a box or tub of rolled fondant. I find Satin Ice to be the best-tasting brand. Duff fondant, found in Michaels craft store, is a good brand. Wilton also makes a fondant readily available in most craft stores. Check the Supplies list for tips and check the Resources section for where to buy. I've provided a fondant recipe just in case you prefer homemade or are unable to find premade fondant.

Fondant. No matter what the naysayers may say, I say fondant is essential in edible crafting. Fondant gives a smooth, finished look to your sweet, is an ideal tool for adding decorations and is very versatile. Fondant is almost perfect, except that I and most others find its super-sugary taste far less delicious than royal icing and buttercream frosting. Even homemade versions of fondant are supersweet. Hence, the controversy. Often, you can substitute candy clay (which is found later in this chapter) or different candies, such as fruit leather, Tootsie Rolls and fruit chews, for fondant decorations, but none are quite as pliable. Further, working with small pieces of candy is more time-consuming than rolling out a large piece of fondant.

Here you'll find a recipe for fondant (or rolled fondant icing), though I highly recommend purchasing premade, white, rolled fondant. The shortcut recipe for marshmallow fondant that follows is a nice compromise between homemade and store-bought, and many people prefer the taste of marshmallow fondant to any other.

If you are using fondant only sparingly for decorations, for practicing or for small-scale sweets, a craft-store brand, likely Wilton, works well. If you are using fondant to coat sweets completely, especially for serving at a party or event, I recommend using a finer brand, such as Satin Ice or Duff. See the Supplies section for tips on which brands are best, and the Resources section for tips on where to buy.

tip

The recipe for fondant calls for about eight cups of confectioners' sugar, or about a two-pound bag. But be sure to purchase extra, as you will need additional confectioners' sugar when working with the fondant to prevent sticking. Use clear vanilla extract in the fondant and marshmallow fondant recipes, if possible, or add white food coloring to brighten the fondant.

Rolled Fondant Icing (aka Fondant)

1 tablespoon (1 packet) unflavored gelatin
3 tablespoons cold water
½ cup light corn syrup
2 tablespoons vegetable shortening (such as Crisco)
1 tablespoon glycerin (found in the craft store)
1 teaspoon clear vanilla extract*
7 to 8 cups (about 2 pounds) confectioners' sugar, plus more for dusting

*You may substitute regular vanilla extract, but note you will need to add additional white food coloring for a bright white fondant.

1. Combine gelatin and cold water in a small bowl and let stand until thick, about 3 minutes. Pour mixture in the top of a double boiler or in a heatproof bowl placed on top of a saucepan with simmering water, and stir until melted. Add light corn syrup and mix well. Stir in shortening until almost melted, and remove from heat. Add glycerin and vanilla extract and stir well. Place 6 cups of the confectioners' sugar in the bowl of a standing mixer fitted with the flat beater. Pour in the gelatin mixture and blend on low until a sticky ball forms. (Instead of a standing mixer, you may use a wooden spoon to stir.)

2. Grease a spatula with shortening and scrape the fondant onto a surface dusted with confectioners' sugar. Knead an additional 1 to 2 cups of confectioners' sugar into the fondant until it is smooth and pliable. Wrap any unused fondant well in plastic to store.

Marshmallow Fondant

Use this shortcut recipe in place of rolled fondant icing anytime a craft calls for fondant. To cover a cake, you will need two batches.

vegetable shortening (such as Crisco)

2 cups mini marshmallows

2 tablespoons water

2 teaspoons clear vanilla extract*

3½ cups confectioners' sugar, plus more for dusting

*You may substitute regular vanilla extract, but note you will need to add additional white food coloring for a bright white fondant.

1. Grease a large microwave-safe bowl with Crisco. Pour marshmallows, water and vanilla extract in bowl. Heat the marshmallows in the microwave until they puff a bit, about 20 to 30 seconds. Stir well until fully melted, smooth and runny.

2. Grease the bowl of your standing mixture or a large mixing bowl. Put the confectioners' sugar in the greased bowl. If using a standing mixer, grease the flat beater well with Crisco, or grease the beaters of a hand mixer well. Gradually pour the marshmallow mixture into the sugar and blend well on low speed until a dough forms. If the mixture is too dry and crumbly, add a teaspoon of water. If mixture is too wet, add ¼ cup of confectioners' sugar. When you have a good, pliable, dough-like mixture, knead briefly on a surface dusted with confectioners' sugar. Wrap fondant in plastic and let sit about half an hour at room temperature.

3. Store unused fondant at room temperature, wrapped very well in plastic.

gum paste vs. fondant

For those wondering about the difference between gum paste and fondant, gum paste is similar to fondant in texture and you work with it in much the same way. But while fondant stiffens, it never becomes rock solid. Gum paste does. Thus, gum paste is not used for covering sweets, only for decorations that have to hold their shape, such as three-dimensional objects. Because gum paste is used sparingly, and is not too fun to eat, I don't use it at all. But if you'd like to dabble with it, I recommend using a store-bought, premixed gum paste from the craft store, or purchase a gum paste mix to prepare at home.

chocolate, candy melts and candy clay

Chocolate and candy melts make a great addition to edible crafting. Melt chocolate or candy melts in a frosting bag and you can pipe away (see the Crazy Chocolate Lollipops). Pipe designs on wax paper, let them set well, and use them to decorate sweets. The craft store carries many different candy and lollipop molds for one-step edible art. Simply fill molds with melted chocolate or candy melts and let set. Or, use chocolate and candy melts to make candy clay and tasty decorations.

Found in the craft store, specialty stores and online, candy melts come in all kinds of colors and flavors. Check the Supplies list for more information on candy melts and the Resources section for tips on where to buy. You may also tint white chocolate and white candy melts different colors with oil-based food coloring. Learn more about this later, in the Techniques section.

> ### tip
> Don't be afraid to add vegetable shortening to your candy melts. Easily dippable candy melts will save you much frustration, I promise.

Melting chocolate and candy melts.
Melt both chocolate chips and candy melts in either the microwave or on the stove top. Choose any microwave-safe bowl, though silicone or plastic work best as they withstand heat well. You do not want to overheat chocolate or candy melts when melting, or you will have a hardened mess. You may also melt them directly in a disposable decorating bag in the microwave. For melting on the stove top, if you do not have a double boiler, rest a heat-safe bowl, such as a stainless-steel bowl, over a saucepan of simmering water. Do not let the water touch the bottom of the bowl.

Don't add any water or other liquid to the melted chocolate or candy melts. If you need to thin for a better consistency, which I almost always do, especially when working with candy melts for dipping sweets, add up to a tablespoon of vegetable shortening, such as Crisco, a little bit at a time. I work with two cups of chocolate chips or one pound (one bag) of candy melts at a time, but you may halve this if you don't need that much. You may put melted chocolate in the refrigerator to set, but do not refrigerate melted candy melts. Let them set at room temperature.

To melt chocolate or candy melts on the stove top: Place two cups of chocolate chips or one pound (one bag) of candy melts in the top of a double boiler or in a heat-safe bowl sitting over a saucepan of simmering water. Stir occasionally. When most of the chocolate chips or candy melts appear shiny and start to melt, stir constantly. When most of the chips or melts are fully melted, remove from heat and stir until completely melted.

To melt chocolate in the microwave: Place chocolate chips in a microwave-safe bowl,

uncovered, or fill a disposable frosting bag half-way (only about one cup of chips will fit in the bag), with the top folded up so no chocolate leaks out of the opening. Microwave for one minute on 70 percent power. Stir the chips or knead the frosting bag. Continue microwaving at 70 percent power for thirty-second intervals, then fifteen-second intervals, until most of the chips are melted. Stir or knead until melted and smooth.

To melt candy melts in the microwave: Follow the same instructions, but use 50 percent power.

Candy Clay.
Candy clay is a yummy, sweet candy made from melted chocolate or candy melts mixed with light corn syrup. You can color candy clay and make shapes, much like when working with fondant. However, while tastier than fondant, candy clay cannot be used on the same scale. While you can roll out candy clay in small amounts, you can't cover sweets with it, as it can crack, and it leaves an oily residue. But it is perfect for making decorations.

While candy clay is very easy to make, it is a bit finicky. You must not add water when making

candy clay or working with it, so be sure to keep your hands and work area dry. Learn more about coloring candy clay and making decorations later, in the Techniques section.

Candy Clay

2 cups semisweet or milk chocolate chips *or*
    1 pound (1 bag) candy melts
⅓ cup light corn syrup

1. Prepare a baking tray lined with wax paper. Melt the chocolate chips or the candy melts according to the previous instructions. As soon as the last chip or melt is melted, stir in the light corn syrup. The mixture will start to thicken immediately. Pour onto the prepared baking tray and spread about an inch thick with a spatula. The mixture will take up only about half of your tray. Let set at room temperature for several hours. Don't skip those hours.

2. After the clay has set, work with small sections at a time. Break off and knead a piece of candy clay with your hands until pliable and moldable. The clay will feel dry at first, but it will soften the more you knead.

3. Store well wrapped in plastic for up to several weeks at room temperature.

> ### tip
> Prepare candy clay with white candy melts; then you may tint the candy clay various colors with oil-based food coloring, also called candy colors.

PART THREE

The Crafts

You can craft sweets into anything imaginable. The ideas here are just a sampling of the possibilities.

Each craft opens with a list of the recipes, supplies and techniques you need so you can quickly reference these in Part One, Two and Four. Every recipe listed is found in this book, but you can almost always substitute your own favorite recipe or store-bought products. I especially recommend using store-bought fondant. I say this repeatedly throughout the book. "Use store-bought fondant!"

The supplies lists pertain mostly to decorating, rather than baking, because I assume you have the basic kitchen tools for baking, such as measuring cups, mixing bowls, a standing or handheld mixer, parchment paper, spatulas, whisks, baking trays, cupcake tins and similar items. Be sure to read the recipes before you begin, though, to make sure you have all the proper tools on hand. I always list specialty baking equipment you may need to purchase, such

as cookie cutters or cupcake liners. You'll find detailed lists of ingredients, baking supplies and decorating tools in Part One. A lot of information is packed in these lists. Pay particular attention to the section on food coloring in Part One. For each craft, I give you the exact names of the AmeriColor gel paste food colors used, my preferred brand. You may choose your own colors and brands, but this will be useful for beginners.

The techniques lists refer to the instructions you'll find in Part Four. The instructions will help you every step of the way, and it's important to refer to these to prevent slipups that might slow you down. So that you can easily find the technique, the full title is listed. For example, you might be asked to check out the technique "Mix color into icing and frosting" even though you are mixing color only into icing.

tip

Remember that most crafts need to dry overnight, and some need to dry overnight between steps, so be sure to plan accordingly!

FLOWERS
&
BUGS

fancy
MARSHMALLOW POPS

1. Measure the height and circumference of a marshmallow. With the scissors, cut out strips from the icing sheets so the width and length match the height and circumference measurements, respectively. Use a pencil to lightly mark the edible icing sheet before cutting, if it helps you.

2. Work with one marshmallow at a time. Hold a marshmallow with your forefinger and thumb at the top and bottom. Use the paintbrush to completely coat the sides of the marshmallow with a thin layer of light corn syrup. Peel the icing sheet strip and carefully wrap the strip around the marshmallow, snipping the ends with scissors if necessary. Smooth with your fingers.

3. Insert a lollipop stick.

stamped bug
COOKIES

Recipes

- ☐ cookies (page 21)
- ☐ poured sugar icing (page 30)

Supplies

- ☐ oval cookie or fondant cutter*
- ☐ gel paste food coloring (white)**
- ☐ wire rack
- ☐ baking tray

Supplies (cont'd)

- ☐ parchment paper
- ☐ rubber bug stamps***
- ☐ edible writers (black, red, blue, yellow and green)

*Use any preferred size cookie cutter as long as it can accommodate your stamps.

**Bright White used here.

***Mini bug stamps by Hero Arts used here, but you may use any bug stamps.

Techniques

- ☐ mix color into icing and frosting
- ☐ coat with poured sugar icing
- ☐ stamp with food coloring
- ☐ use edible writers

1. Roll out, cut out and bake oval cookies according to the recipe. Let cool completely.

2. Prepare poured sugar icing according to the recipe and tint white.

3. Place the wire rack on a baking tray lined with parchment paper. Arrange the cookies on the wire rack and coat with poured sugar icing according to the technique instructions. Let dry overnight.

4. Follow the instructions for stamping with food coloring using your edible writers and rubber stamps. Stamp the bugs with black; then use the red, blue, yellow and green edible writers to sketch in highlights of color.

shortcut and tip

Skip sketching in highlights of color and rather than black, just use one bright color for the stamp.

critters on a stick
COOKIES

Recipes

- ☐ cookies (chocolate suggested) (page 22)
- ☐ royal icing (page 29)

Supplies

- ☐ cookie stick template
- ☐ gel paste food coloring (brown)*
- ☐ 2 decorating bags
- ☐ coupler
- ☐ decorating tip, size 4
- ☐ rubber band
- ☐ palette
- ☐ small liner paintbrush

*Chocolate Brown used here.

Techniques

- ☐ mix color into icing and frosting
- ☐ assemble a decorating bag
- ☐ pipe with a decorating bag
- ☐ flood royal icing
- ☐ paint with food coloring

1. Roll out your chilled cookie dough and cut the sticks with the template, or just cut long rectangles. Bake according to the recipe and let cool completely.

2. Prepare royal icing according to the recipe and tint light brown. Prepare a decorating bag with size 4 decorating tip and fill with half of your icing. Close the bag tightly with a rubber band. Cover and reserve remaining icing.

3. Pipe an outline on the cookies with the icing. Use the remaining empty decorating bag to flood the cookies with the reserved light brown icing according to the technique instructions, and let dry for several hours, though overnight is preferred.

4. Mix a few drops of water with a drop of brown food coloring in your palette. Paint thin, wavy lines, according to the technique instructions, for a wood grain.

Candy Clay Critter Toppers

Recipes

- □ candy clay (page 35)

Techniques

- □ mix color into candy clay
- □ make candy clay decorations
- □ use sprinkles and candy
- □ use edible writers

Supplies

- □ white candy melts
- □ oil-based food coloring (green, yellow, black and red candy colors)
- □ black edible writer
- □ toothpick
- □ light corn syrup
- □ large confetti sprinkles

ideas

- You can also make the candy clay bugs with fondant, but be sure to use gel paste coloring, not the oil-based candy colors.

- Use these bugs to decorate cupcakes, petits fours and cakes. You may also use these on the Fairy Woodland Petits Fours in this book.

1. Prepare candy clay according to the recipe using white candy melts.

2. Divide and color your candy clay. For the bugs, you'll need lime green (add drops of both green and yellow coloring), yellow, black and red.

3. **To make the worm,** roll 5 pieces of lime green clay into balls and gently press on counter to slightly flatten one side. Balls should be roughly the size of peas, but make each ball progressively smaller. Draw 2 dots for eyes on the largest ball. Use a toothpick to dab light corn syrup between each ball to adhere in a row and arrange on the cookie stick.

For the bee, roll a pea-size ball of black clay and a yellow ball about twice as big and slightly flatten the underside of each. Use the tip of a black edible writer to draw black lines on the yellow ball. Insert 2 confetti sprinkles into the top of the yellow ball for wings. Attach the head to the yellow ball with light corn syrup and arrange on the cookie stick.

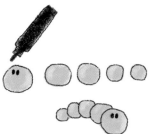

For the ladybug, roll a pea-size ball of black and a red ball about twice as big and flatten the underside of each. Draw dots on the red with the edible writer. Adhere the head to the body with a dab of light corn syrup and arrange on the cookie stick.

shortcuts

Use store-bought cake mix and frosting. Or omit the buttercream frosting and just use the royal icing to top cupcakes before adding the fondant. You may also skip piping the dots, so there is no need for the royal icing, decorating bag, coupler, tip and rubber band, though you will need either frosting or icing to attach the fondant to the cupcakes.

lazy daisy
CUPCAKES

Recipes

- ☐ cupcakes (page 24)
- ☐ buttercream frosting (page 30)
- ☐ fondant (store-bought recommended) (page 32)
- ☐ royal icing (page 29)

Supplies

- ☐ cupcake liners
- ☐ gel paste food coloring (turquoise, red and yellow)*
- ☐ rolling pin
- ☐ confectioners' sugar

Supplies (cont'd)

- ☐ 3-inch circle cookie cutter
- ☐ spatula or knife
- ☐ 1½-inch and/or 2½-inch daisy fondant cutters
- ☐ ½-inch circle fondant cutter
- ☐ toothpick
- ☐ light corn syrup
- ☐ decorating bag
- ☐ coupler
- ☐ decorating tip, size 2
- ☐ rubber band

*Turquoise, Red Red and Egg Yellow used here.

Techniques

- ☐ mix color into icing and frosting
- ☐ mix color into fondant
- ☐ cover sweets with fondant
- ☐ make fondant decorations
- ☐ assemble a decorating bag
- ☐ pipe with a decorating bag

1. Prepare cupcakes according to the recipe and let cool completely.

2. Prepare buttercream frosting according to the recipe. Leave untinted or tint turquoise.

3. Prepare fondant, divide and tint turquoise, red and yellow. You'll need mostly turquoise, as this is your background color, a smaller batch of red and only a little of yellow.

4. Roll the turquoise fondant on a surface dusted with confectioners' sugar. Cut out circles with the 3-inch cutter, spread buttercream frosting on the cupcakes with a spatula or knife and top with fondant circles according to the technique instructions.

5. Roll out both the red and yellow fondant. Cut out red daisies with the 1½-inch or 2½-inch fondant cutters and yellow circles with the ½-inch circle cutter. Use a toothpick to add a dab of corn syrup to the back of the yellow circles and adhere to the center of the red daisies. Using corn syrup as glue, adhere the daisy to the fondant on the cupcake, smoothing with your fingers.

6. Prepare royal icing according to the recipe, and tint red. Assemble a decorating bag with the coupler and size 2 tip, fill with icing and close tightly with a rubber band.

7. Pipe dots on the cupcakes. Let dry for several hours or overnight.

pretty painted
PETITS FOURS

Recipes

- □ petits fours (page 26)
- □ buttercream frosting (page 30)
- □ fondant (store-bought recommended) (page 32)

Supplies

- □ 1½-inch to 2½-inch square cookie or fondant cutter*
- □ gel paste food coloring (pink, green and white)**
- □ rolling pin
- □ palette
- □ small round paintbrush
- □ small liner paintbrush

*Use any preferred square or circle cutter in this size range.

**Electric Pink, Electric Green and Bright White used here.

Techniques

- □ mix color into fondant
- □ cover sweets with fondant
- □ paint with food coloring

idea

Use this design on fondant, flooded icing or poured sugar icing to top cupcakes, cookies or cakes.

shortcut

Substitute snack cakes or frozen pound cake for the petits fours, and use store-bought frosting. You may not need frosting if you are using a sticky snack cake, such as an Oreo Cakester.

1. Bake and cut out the petits fours according to the recipe and let cool completely.

2. Prepare buttercream frosting according to the recipe.

3. Prepare fondant, and if needed, brighten with white food coloring. If using store-bought white fondant, you won't need additional coloring.

4. If desired, stack two petits fours with buttercream frosting between the layers, or just use one layer. Frost the petits fours with a thin layer of buttercream frosting. Roll out the fondant and cover the petits fours according to the technique instructions.

5. Prepare food coloring on the palette. You'll need light pink, hot pink and lime green. For light pink, mix a drop of Electric Pink, a few drops of Bright White and a few drops of water. For hot pink, mix a drop of Electric Pink with a few drops of water. For lime green, mix a drop of Electric Green, a few drops of Bright White and a few drops of water.

6. With the small round brush, paint light pink circles and let set about 10 minutes. With the liner brush, paint a swirl of hot pink on top. Use either brush to draw and fill leaves with lime green coloring.

hyacinth
COOKIE POPS

Recipes

- ☐ cookies (page 21)
- ☐ buttercream frosting (page 30)
- ☐ melting chocolate and candy melts (page 34)

Supplies

- ☐ 1½-inch circle cookie or fondant cutter
- ☐ cookie or lollipop sticks
- ☐ gel paste food coloring (purple, green and white)*

Supplies (cont'd)

- ☐ 2 decorating bags
- ☐ 2 couplers
- ☐ 2 decorating tips, closed star tips size 30**
- ☐ rubber bands
- ☐ palette
- ☐ paintbrush
- ☐ wax or parchment paper
- ☐ purple candy melts
- ☐ Styrofoam block

*Electric Purple, Electric Green and Bright White used here.

**Try any comparable textured tip for a different look.

Techniques

- ☐ put sweets on sticks
- ☐ mix color into icing and frosting
- ☐ dip sweets in candy melts
- ☐ assemble a decorating bag
- ☐ pipe with a decorating bag

idea

Make these cookie pops in a mix of colors: blue, purple and pink. Just use coordinating colors of candy melts and gel pastes.

1. Roll out chilled cookie dough, cut out circles and insert sticks according to the recipe. Bake and let cool completely.

2. Prepare buttercream frosting according to the recipe, divide in half and tint 2 shades of purple. Assemble decorating bags with couplers and tips, fill with your frosting shades and close tightly with a rubber band.

3. Mix a couple of drops of green and a few drops of white food coloring on a palette or on a piece of wax paper. Paint the lollipop sticks and let dry, resting the pops on a flat surface lined with parchment or wax paper.

4. Melt purple candy melts according to the technique instructions, dip your cookie pops, and then prop in a Styrofoam block. Let the candy melts set well.

5. Lay the cookies on a piece of parchment or wax paper. Pipe dots with the star tip in both colors of purple to cover a cookie. When you have covered as much of the cookie as possible, lift it by the stick with one hand and pipe around the edge of the cookie with your other hand. Prop in a Styrofoam block. Repeat for the remaining cookies.

tip

This is one of the few instances in this book where we use textured decorating tips to pipe butter-cream frosting, a technique used primarily in cake decorating. But this is a great way to practice using more advanced decorating tips, since these cookie pops are so easy to decorate.

flower
CAKE POPS

Recipes

- ☐ cake pops (cake and buttercream frosting) (page 25)
- ☐ melting chocolate and candy melts (page 34)

Supplies

- ☐ green food coloring
- ☐ palette or wax paper
- ☐ paintbrush
- ☐ lollipop sticks

Supplies (cont'd)

- ☐ yellow candy melts
- ☐ yellow sprinkles
- ☐ Styrofoam block
- ☐ pencil
- ☐ 3-inch daisy cookie cutter (or use the template)
- ☐ brightly colored or printed card stock
- ☐ scissors
- ☐ toothpick or pin
- ☐ green card stock
- ☐ leaf template
- ☐ glue stick

Techniques

- ☐ put sweets on sticks
- ☐ dip sweets in candy melts
- ☐ use sprinkles and candy

idea and shortcut

In lieu of cake pops, dip a marshmallow in water, and then immediately coat with yellow sprinkles.

1. Pour a few drops of green food coloring on a palette or piece of wax paper. Carefully use the paintbrush to paint lollipop sticks green and set aside on wax paper to dry completely.

2. Follow the recipe for cake pops to bake your cake, prepare your cake balls and chill.

3. Melt yellow candy melts according to the instructions. Working with one cake pop at a time, dip the tip of your lollipop stick in the candy melts, insert into a chilled cake ball, and dip cake ball in the candy melts. Hold the cake pop over a bowl or plate and sprinkle sprinkles generously over it to coat completely. Stand the cake pop in a Styrofoam block to set well.

4. Trace the daisy cookie cutter or use the template to draw a flower on the brightly colored or printed card stock. Cut out the flower and make a hole in the center with a toothpick or a pin. Fold green card stock, hold the leaf template against the fold (don't cut the fold), and cut out the leaf shape.

5. Slide the flower cutout on the stick under the cake pop. Unfold and glue the entire inside of the leaf, including the band. Wrap the leaf around the stick just under the flower. This will help keep the paper cutout from sliding down the stick. If desired, add another leaf. Let the glue dry.

pile of posies
CAKE

Recipes

- ☐ fondant (store-bought recom-mended) (page 32)
- ☐ cake (page 24)
- ☐ buttercream frosting (2 batches) (page 30)

Supplies

- ☐ gel paste food coloring (green, blue, and yellow)*
- ☐ baking tray
- ☐ wax paper
- ☐ rolling pin
- ☐ confectioners' sugar

Supplies (cont'd)

- ☐ 3 flower fondant or cookie cutters (2-inch and 3-inch)
- ☐ ½-inch circle fondant cutter
- ☐ toothpick
- ☐ light corn syrup
- ☐ assorted candy**
- ☐ 2 leaf fondant cutters (1-inch and 1½-inch)
- ☐ offset spatula

*Sky Blue, Egg Yellow and Electric Green used here.

**This is used only to help shape the flowers. Candy corn, mini gumdrops or other small candies work well.

Techniques

- ☐ mix color into fondant
- ☐ make fondant decorations
- ☐ mix color into icing and frosting
- ☐ frost cakes

1. Prepare fondant, divide and tint lime green and 2 shades of blue.

2. Prepare a baking tray lined with wax paper. Roll out each shade of blue fondant ¼-inch thick on a surface dusted with confectioners' sugar. Cut out flowers in a mixture of the 3 sizes, and cut out a ½-inch circle in a contrasting blue for each daisy. Use a toothpick or your finger to dab light corn syrup on the underside of the circle and adhere to the daisy. Arrange each flower on the baking tray. Push some up against the side of the tray and drape some over 2 or 3 pieces of candy

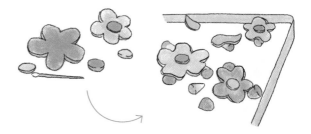

corn or comparable candy to give the flowers shape. Roll out and cut out an assortment of leaves and arrange on the baking tray just as you did the flowers. For the base of the cake, cut out ½-inch circles in the 2 shades of blue fondant and cut out 1-inch leaves in green and set aside on wax paper (these don't need to be shaped).

To make a 9-inch round cake, for the top of the cake, you'll need 3 large daisies, 6 medium and 10 small, each with a ½-inch circle of fondant in the center, and 8 1½-inch leaves and 8 1-inch leaves. For the ring at the bottom, you'll need about 40 ½-inch circles and 32 1-inch leaves. But it doesn't hurt to have extra, just in case.

3. Bake your cake and let cool completely.

4. Prepare buttercream frosting according to the recipe and tint light yellow.

5. Frost your cake according to the technique instructions. You'll use about 1½ batches of frosting for the middle layer, crumb coat and final coat.

6. Immediately after frosting your cake, add the fondant decorations. If any pieces have trouble sticking, use a dab of frosting to adhere. Layer the flowers as desired, inserting leaves. Make a ring around the bottom with ½-inch circles and 1-inch leaves.

ANIMALS
&
OUTDOORS

fairy woodland
PETITS FOURS

Recipes

- ☐ petits fours (page 26)
- ☐ buttercream frosting (page 30)
- ☐ fondant (store-bought recommended) (page 32)

Supplies

- ☐ 2¼-inch circle cookie or fondant cutter*
- ☐ gel paste food coloring (brown)**
- ☐ rolling pin
- ☐ confectioners' sugar
- ☐ tape measure
- ☐ palette
- ☐ small liner paintbrush
- ☐ candy clay bugs (page 46)
- ☐ mini fondant flowers (page 57)
- ☐ light corn syrup

*Use any comparably sized circle cutter.

**Chocolate Brown used here.

Techniques

- ☐ mix color into icing and frosting
- ☐ mix color into fondant
- ☐ cover sweets with fondant
- ☐ make fondant decorations
- ☐ paint with food coloring

tip

Depending on how many tree stumps you make, you may need at least two boxes of store-bought fondant or two batches of homemade. Each tree stump requires at least an egg-size piece of fondant.

shortcut

Use store-bought frozen pound cake and frosting for the petits fours.

1. Prepare petits fours according to the recipe and cut out 2¼-inch circles.

2. Prepare buttercream frosting according to the recipe and either tint brown to match the fondant or leave untinted. Cover and reserve.

3. Prepare fondant, divide and tint 2 colors, light brown and dark brown. You will need significantly more of the dark brown fondant.

4. Stack 2 to 3 petit four circles with layers of buttercream frosting. Roll out the light brown fondant on a surface dusted with confectioners' sugar. Cut out 2¼-inch circles. Frost the

top of a stacked petit four with buttercream frosting and top with a fondant circle. Roll out a long strip of dark brown fondant. Measure the height of the petit four, including the light brown fondant circle. Cut a strip from the dark brown fondant that is just a bit longer than the circumference of the petit four and as wide as your measured height, plus an additional ¼ inch. Frost the sides of the petit four. Wrap the strip around the petit four so the top edge is flush with the top of the light brown circle. Smooth the sides and seal by pressing the fondant edges together. With your fingers, stretch and pull a few sections of the fondant on the bottom and pinch to create the roots of the tree stump. Tuck the rest of the edges under the bottom of the petit four.

5. Pour a drop or two of brown food coloring on the palette and mix with a few drops of water. Use the liner paintbrush to paint a wood grain: thin, wavy lines on the sides of the tree stump, and wavy circles on the top.

6. Decorate the tree stump with candy clay bugs or mini fondant flowers, as shown in the Pile of Posies Cake photo. (Note: you may make the candy clay bugs with fondant and gel paste coloring in lieu of candy clay and oil-based colors.) Adhere decorations with dabs of light corn syrup and let dry.

Toadstool marshmallows

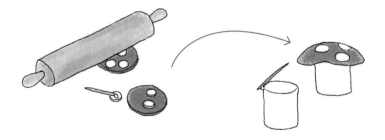

Recipes

- ☐ fondant (store-bought recommended) (page 32)

Supplies

- ☐ gel paste food coloring (red, white)*
- ☐ rolling pin
- ☐ 2¼-inch circle cookie or fondant cutter

Supplies (cont'd)

- ☐ confectioners' sugar
- ☐ ½-inch circle cookie or fondant cutter
- ☐ toothpick
- ☐ light corn syrup
- ☐ marshmallows
- ☐ wax paper

*Red Red and Bright White used here. Store-bought white fondant may not need additional white coloring.

Techniques

- ☐ mix color into fondant
- ☐ make fondant decorations

idea

Display the tree stumps and Toadstool Marshmallows on a bed of faux grass or moss as part of a fairy-themed dessert table.

1. Prepare fondant, divide and tint red. You'll also need white fondant.

2. Roll out the red fondant and cut out a 2¼-inch circle for each toadstool. Roll out white fondant on a surface dusted with confectioners' sugar. Cut out ½-inch circles, 3 to 4 per toadstool. Top each red circle with 3 to 4 white circles, using a toothpick to dab light corn syrup on the underside of the white circles to adhere. Briefly and gently roll the red circles with a rolling pin to smush the white dots so that they stick.

3. Sit a marshmallow on its flat end on the counter. Dab light corn syrup around the edges of the marshmallow's top with a toothpick or your finger. Center a red circle on top of the marshmallow, and gently press the fondant edges around the top of the marshmallow so they drape a bit. Set toadstools aside on wax paper to stiffen.

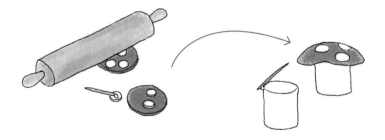

swamp frog
CUPCAKES

Recipes

- ☐ fondant (store-bought recommended) (page 32)
- ☐ cupcakes (page 24)
- ☐ buttercream frosting (page 30)

Supplies

- ☐ gel paste food coloring (blue, two shades of green, and white)*
- ☐ rolling pin
- ☐ confectioners' sugar
- ☐ 2½-inch circle cookie cutter

Supplies (cont'd)

- ☐ knife
- ☐ wax paper
- ☐ light corn syrup
- ☐ black edible writer
- ☐ toothpick
- ☐ cupcake liners
- ☐ disposable decorating bag
- ☐ coupler
- ☐ decorating tip, size 12
- ☐ rubber band

*Electric Green (for the frog) and Leaf Green (for the lily pad) used here. Sky Blue and Bright White also used. If using store-bought white fondant, you won't need the Bright White coloring.

Techniques

- ☐ mix color into icing and frosting
- ☐ assemble a decorating bag
- ☐ pipe with a decorating bag
- ☐ frost cupcakes
- ☐ mix color into fondant
- ☐ make fondant decorations
- ☐ use edible writers

tip
You may want to use a larger decorating bag to pipe the frosting on the cupcakes.

1. Prepare fondant, divide and tint. You will need a little bit of white and two shades of green. Use Leaf Green for the lily pad and Electric Green for the frog.

2. Roll out the leaf green fondant on a surface dusted with confectioners' sugar. Cut out 2½-inch circles. Cut a wedge from each circle with a knife, and set the lily pad aside on wax paper to stiffen several hours or overnight.

3. To make your froggies, you will need lime green fondant (made with Electric Green gel paste) and white fondant. For each frog you will need 2 green pea-size balls (¼-inch diameter), 2 green balls ⅛-inch in diameter, 1 green 1-inch ball and 2 white ⅛-inch balls. Smush and pinch the pea-size green balls into flattened ovals. Flatten the ⅛-inch green balls into circles. Arrange on the counter as shown. These are the feet. Flatten one side

of the 1-inch ball a bit, dab corn syrup on the flattened side and press on top of the feet. Adhere the white balls on top of the green ball with dabs of corn syrup. With the edible writer, draw 2 dots for eyes and either a large frown or a large smile. Use a toothpick to dab corn syrup under the feet and stick the frog on a lily pad.

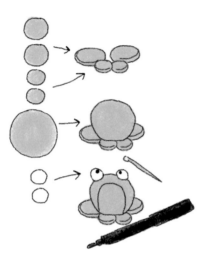

4. Prepare cupcakes according to the recipe, bake and let cool.

5. Prepare frosting according to the recipe and tint blue. Prepare a decorating bag with the coupler and size 12 tip, fill with the frosting and close tightly with a rubber band.

6. Pipe to frost the cupcakes according to the technique instructions.

7. Right before serving, place a lily pad with a frog on top of a frosted cupcake.

tips

• If you are using store-bought frosting, thicken it with some confectioners' sugar. If the frosting is not stiff enough, the weight of the cupcake topper may smush it.

• You may want to use a larger decorating bag to pipe the frosting on the cupcakes.

farm animal
SNACK CAKES

Recipes

- petits fours* (page 26)
- buttercream frosting (page 30)
- fondant (store-bought recommended) (page 32)

*Oreo Cakesters used here instead of petits fours and frosting.

Supplies

- 2½-inch circle cookie or fondant cutter*
- gel paste food coloring (pink, white, yellow, black and orange)**
- rolling pin

Supplies (cont'd)

- confectioners' sugar
- 1¼-inch circle cookie or fondant cutter
- toothpick
- light corn syrup
- knife
- ½-inch circle fondant cutter
- black edible writer

*Use any comparable size circle cutter and adjust any of the decorations as needed. If using store-bought snack cakes, you won't need the 2½-inch cutter.

**Electric Pink, Bright White, Egg Yellow, Super Black and Orange used here. If using store-bought white fondant, you won't need the white coloring.

Techniques

- mix color into fondant
- cover sweets with fondant
- make fondant decorations
- use edible writers

idea

You can also use this method for cookie pops. Either top cookies with circles of fondant or use royal icing to flood a white or pink background and add fondant decorations.

1. Bake petits fours according to the recipe and cut 2½-inch circles. Or just unwrap a store-bought snack cake like I do here.

2. If you are using homemade petits fours or snack cakes that aren't sticky, you'll need to prepare buttercream frosting.

3. Prepare fondant, divide and tint your colors. You'll need light pink, white, dark pink, yellow, black and orange fondant. You'll need a good deal of light pink and white, for the background colors.

4. If desired, stack two petits fours with a layer of frosting between, or use one layer. Frost the petits fours. Oreo Cakesters will not need frosting. Roll out white fondant (for the cows and ducks) and light pink fondant (for the pigs) on a surface dusted with confectioners' sugar, and wrap petits fours or snack cakes according to the technique instructions.

5. **For the pig,** roll out the darker pink fondant and cut out a 1¼-inch circle. Use a toothpick or your finger to dab light corn syrup on the back of the circle and adhere it to a light pink petit four, centered at the bottom. Take 2 pea-size pieces (¼-inch diameter) of light pink fondant and pinch into triangles. Use a toothpick or your finger to dab light corn syrup on the underside of the triangles and adhere to the sides of the petit four for ears.

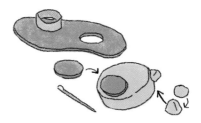

For the duck, roll out the orange fondant and use a knife to cut out the shape shown. Adhere to the center of the petit four with corn syrup.

For the cow, roll out light pink fondant and cut out a ½-inch circle for the snout. Attach to the lower half of the petit four with corn syrup. Roll out black fondant and use a knife to cut out bloblike pieces as shown. Adhere to the petit four with corn syrup. Pinch 2 pea-size white balls of fondant into triangles and adhere to the sides of the petit four for ears. Pinch 2 pea-size yellow balls of fondant into triangles with the tops bent in and adhere to the sides of the petit four for horns. Stand the pig and cow upright against the rolling pin to let the ears and horns dry.

6. With the black edible writer, draw eyes and nostrils for the pig, draw eyes and 2 lines on the beak for the duck, and draw eyes and nostrils for the cow.

lawn ornament
CAKE

idea

Decorate a cake or cupcakes with gnomes and flamingos for a housewarming or garden party. I used a six-inch cake here, but you may also use a nine-inch cake or cupcakes.

shortcut

Use store-bought cake mix and frosting.

1. Prepare fondant, divide and tint. You will need the following colors: red, peach, blue, black, pink and white. To make peach fondant, add only a tiny drop to start.

2. To make your flamingo, roll a ball of pink fondant 1 inch in diameter. Pinch one end to flatten, and curl it up a bit. Roll a ½-inch ball of pink fondant into a 2-inch log. Bend into an S shape, dab corn syrup on one end and press into the front of the pinched ball. Rest the flamingo on its side on wax paper. Insert 2 toothpicks in the underside of the flamingo for legs. Roll a pea-size ball (¼-inch diameter)

of white fondant and pinch it into a cone. Dab a bit of corn syrup on the flat end and press

it onto the other end of the pink S. Let the flamingo sit on its side to dry several hours or overnight. When dry, use the black edible writer to add eyes and to color the tip of the beak.

3. **For each gnome** you will need

    head: a ¾-inch peach ball, flattened slightly on the top and bottom

    hands: 2 pea-size (¼-inch diameter) peach balls, flattened slightly on the top and bottom

    nose: a half pea-size (⅛-inch diameter) peach ball

    feet: 2 ½-inch black balls, flattened and pinched slightly into oval loaves

    body: a 1-inch blue ball, flattened slightly on the top and bottom

    arms: 2 pea-size (¼-inch diameter) blue balls

    hat: a ½-inch ball of red, pinched into a cone

    beard: a pea-size (¼-inch diameter) ball of white

4. Using a light dab of corn syrup as glue for each piece, line up the 2 black feet. Rest the body on top. Sit the head on top of the body. Roll each arm into a ½-inch log and pinch one end to flatten. Attach to the side of the gnome and press a hand at each end against the gnome's body. Attach the nose to the face. Press the beard between your forefinger and thumb and attach beneath the nose. Make an indent with your finger on the flat side of the red cone and attach to the top of the gnome's head. Make 2 eyes with the black edible writer. Let the gnome dry several hours or overnight. Lay him down to rest if necessary.

5. Bake your cake according to the recipe and let cool completely.

6. Prepare buttercream frosting and tint lime green with gel paste food coloring.

7. Tint coconut in a sealable bag with a few drops of lime green gel paste food coloring according to the technique instructions.

8. Frost your cake according to the technique instructions. Immediately sprinkle and press the coconut on the top of the cake.

9. Insert flamingo(s) in the cake and place gnome(s) where desired.

animal print
COOKIE POPS

Recipes

- ☐ cookies (page 21)
- ☐ royal icing (page 29)
- ☐ fondant (store-bought recommended) (page 32)

Supplies

- ☐ 2½-inch circle cookie or fondant cutter*
- ☐ cookie or lollipop sticks
- ☐ gel paste food coloring (white, yellow, black and brown)**
- ☐ 4 disposable decorating bags
- ☐ 2 couplers

Supplies (cont'd)

- ☐ 2 decorating tips, size 4
- ☐ rubber bands
- ☐ rolling pin
- ☐ confectioners' sugar
- ☐ pizza cutter
- ☐ toothpick
- ☐ light corn syrup
- ☐ scissors
- ☐ ½-inch circle fondant cutter
- ☐ 1-inch leaf fondant cutter
- ☐ ½-inch square fondant cutter

*Use any comparable size circle.

**Bright White, Egg Yellow, Super Black and Chocolate Brown used here.

Techniques

- ☐ put sweets on sticks
- ☐ mix color into icing and frosting
- ☐ mix color into fondant
- ☐ assemble a decorating bag
- ☐ pipe with a decorating bag
- ☐ flood royal icing
- ☐ make fondant decorations

1. Roll out chilled cookie dough, cut out 2½-inch circles, insert lollipop sticks and bake according to the recipe. Let cool completely.

2. Prepare royal icing according to the recipe, divide and tint 2 colors: white and yellow. Prepare 2 decorating bags with couplers and size 4 tips. Fill each with half of the white and yellow icing and close tightly with rubber bands. Cover the reserved icing.

3. Pipe an outline on each cookie with white (zebras) or yellow (leopards and giraffes) icing. Use the remaining empty decorating bags to flood the backgrounds white or yellow according to the technique instructions. Let set very well, several hours or overnight.

4. Prepare fondant, divide and tint 2 colors: black and brown.

5. **For the zebra,** roll out the black fondant ⅛-inch thick on a surface dusted with confectioners' sugar. Cut out circles with the same cutter you used to cut out the cookies. This will serve as a sizing guide. Use the pizza cutter to cut strips in the circle, moving the cutter in a wave to make curves. Separate the pieces. Use the pizza cutter to slice a couple of the strips in half (with curved lines, not straight across). Use a toothpick to dab light corn syrup on the underside of the strips and adhere the strips, spaced apart, on the white frosted cookies. You won't use all the strips from each circle of black fondant. Snip any excess fondant over the cookie's edge with scissors.

For the leopard, roll out both brown and black fondant. Cut out ½-inch circles of brown and 1-inch leaves of black. Use the ½-inch circle cutter to cut away a piece on the bulbous side of the black leaf. Pick up a brown circle and a black partial leaf, wrap thè partial leaf around the circle, smushing them together a bit and distorting the circle a bit. Adhere to the yellow cookies with corn syrup. Attach small bits of black fondant to the cookies.

For the giraffe, roll out the brown fondant and cut out ½-inch square shapes. Use your fingers to distort the squares a bit and then adhere to the yellow cookies with light corn syrup.

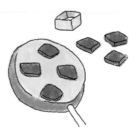

cardinal & birch
COOKIES

Recipes

- ☐ cookies (page 21)
- ☐ poured sugar icing (page 30)
- ☐ fondant (store-bought recommended) (page 32)

Supplies

- ☐ 2½-inch square cookie cutter*
- ☐ gel paste food coloring (blue, red, white and yellow)**
- ☐ wire rack
- ☐ baking tray
- ☐ parchment paper

Supplies (cont'd)

- ☐ rolling pin
- ☐ confectioners' sugar
- ☐ pizza cutter or dough scraper
- ☐ 2-inch leaf fondant cutter
- ☐ knife
- ☐ toothpick
- ☐ light corn syrup
- ☐ black edible writer

*You may use any size cookie cutter, or you may use a circle or oval.

**Sky Blue, Red Red, Bright White and Egg Yellow used here. If using store-bought white fondant, you won't need additional white coloring.

Techniques

- ☐ mix color into icing and frosting
- ☐ coat with poured sugar icing
- ☐ mix color into fondant
- ☐ make fondant decorations
- ☐ use edible writers

idea

These would be perfect at wintertime. Or, choose any color bird and make brown trees. Use light brown fondant and paint a wood grain with the same method used on page 60.

1. Roll out chilled cookie dough, cut out 2½-inch squares and bake according to the recipe. Let cool completely.

2. Prepare poured sugar icing according to the recipe and tint light blue.

3. Place the wire rack on a baking tray lined with parchment paper. Arrange the cookies on the wire rack and coat with poured sugar icing according to the technique instructions. Let dry several hours, preferably overnight.

4. Prepare fondant, divide and tint. You'll need red, white and a little bit of yellow.

5. To make the birch trees, roll out white fondant on a surface dusted with confectioners' sugar. Cut out a square with the same cutter you used to cut out the cookies. This will serve as a sizing guide for your trees. Use the pizza cutter or dough scraper to cut out the tree shape as shown.

6. To make the birds, roll out red fondant and cut out 2-inch leaves with the leaf cutter. Roll out the yellow fondant; cut out triangles for the beaks. Use a toothpick to dab light corn syrup on the beak to attach it to the red leaf.

7. Use a toothpick to dab light corn syrup on the underside of the fondant decorations, and adhere to the cookie, arranging the bird above the branch. Use the black edible writer to draw horizontal lines on the birch tree, an eye on the bird and 2 legs between the bird and the branch.

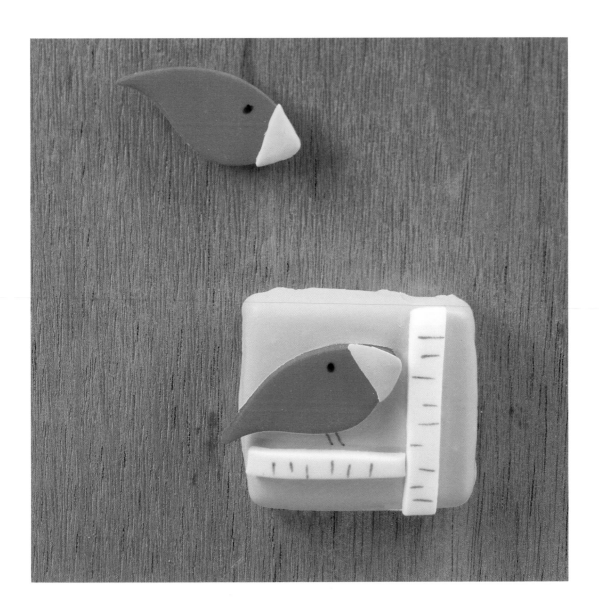

under the sea
CUPCAKES

1. Prepare fondant, divide and tint. To make both creatures, you'll need white, purple and red.

2. **For the octopus,** roll 8 purple balls ½ inch in diameter into 2½-inch logs. Roll a purple ball about 1¼ inch in diameter. Taper the end of the ball a bit with your forefinger and thumb, and flatten the tapered end on the counter. For the eyes, roll out white fondant thinly, ⅛-inch thick, on a surface dusted with confectioners' sugar. Cut out 2 ½-inch circles for each octopus. Roll out purple fondant and cut out 1 ½-inch circle for each octopus. Cut the purple circle in half and attach each half on the upper half of each white circle, using a dab of water or corn syrup. Smush the

rounded edge of the purple semicircle a bit over the top of the white circle. Add a black dot to each with the black edible writer. Use a toothpick to dab corn syrup on the underside of each eye and adhere to the larger purple ball. Set the pieces aside on wax paper.

For each crab, roll a ball of red fondant about 1 inch in diameter. Flatten the top and bottom a bit and pinch to form a slightly flattened oval. Snip 6 pieces of red licorice lace, about 1⅛ inches long. Insert the ends into the sides of the red oval. Roll 2 half pea-size balls of

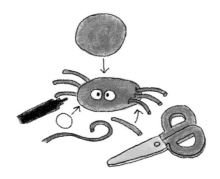

white fondant (about ⅛-inch diameter) and attach to the top of the red oval with corn syrup. Add 2 black dots with the edible writer. Set aside on wax paper.

3. Bake cupcakes in desired liners according to the recipe and let cool.

4. Prepare frosting according to the recipe, divide and tint light blue and light brown.

5. For the sea, spread blue frosting on the cupcake with a spatula, making swirls and peaks. For the sand, spread light brown frosting on the cupcake. Dip the top in white sprinkles or light brown sugar to generously coat.

For the octopus, on the blue frosted cupcakes, arrange the legs first, with one end of each converging at the center of the cupcake, and the other end dangling over the side. Attach the head at the center.

For the crabs, place on top of the "sandy" cupcakes.

SILLY
&
FUN

fruit and veggie
MARSHMALLOW KEBABS

Supplies

- □ 8-inch lollipop sticks
- □ vegetable shortening
- □ marshmallows
- □ edible writers (orange, green, light green, red, purple, blue, yellow and black)

Techniques

- □ put sweets on sticks
- □ use edible writers

1. Grease the top 4 inches of 8-inch lollipop sticks with vegetable shortening. Skewer 4 marshmallows on each stick.

2. Follow the step-by-step instructions below to draw your fruit and veggies with the edible writers.

To draw a carrot, draw and fill a carrot shape with orange. Draw and fill a green pouf at the top. Outline with black and draw lines on the orange.

To draw a radish, draw and almost completely fill a red circle. Draw and fill a big green pouf at the top. Outline with black, making a point at the bottom of the red circle.

To draw peas, draw and fill 3 light green circles. Draw and fill a darker green semi-oval behind the circles. Outline with black. Add a curlicue in green.

To draw an eggplant, draw and fill a green stem with 3 spikes. Draw and fill a purple eggplant shape beneath the green. Outline with black.

To draw a kiwi, draw and fill a light green circle. Draw a thick darker green circle around the light green circle. Outline with black and make a bunch of little lines between the 2 greens.

To draw a blueberry, draw and fill a blue circle. Outline the circle with black and draw a star shape on the circle.

To draw a banana, draw and fill a moon shape with yellow. Outline with black, adding black lines on the banana.

To draw a strawberry, draw and fill a green stem with 3 spikes. Draw and fill a strawberry shape with red. Outline with black and add lines on the red.

swirly
COOKIE BITES

Recipes

☐ cookies (page 21)
☐ royal icing (page 29)

Supplies

☐ 1½ inch circle fondant or cookie cutter*
☐ gel paste food coloring (white, blue, pink, green and orange)**

Supplies (cont'd)

☐ decorating bags***
☐ couplers
☐ decorating tips, size 5
☐ rubber bands
☐ sprinkles to coordinate with icing colors

*Use any preferred size circle.

**Bright White, Sky Blue, Electric Pink, Electric Green and Orange used here.

***You'll need 1 decorating bag, coupler and tip for each color icing you choose, plus 1 of each for white icing.

Techniques

☐ mix color into icing and frosting
☐ assemble a decorating bag
☐ pipe with a decorating bag
☐ use sprinkles and candy

idea

Make these cookies as larger circles on lollipop sticks.

1. Bake 1½-inch circle cookies according to the recipe and let cool completely.

2. Prepare royal icing according to the recipe, divide and tint white and any other colors you prefer. Prepare decorating bags with couplers and size 5 tips, fill with the white and colored icing, and close tightly with rubber bands.

3. Working with one cookie at a time, pipe a swirl with a colored icing. Immediately coat with sprinkles in a coordinating color, and turn over to remove excess.

4. Pipe a white icing swirl on each cookie.

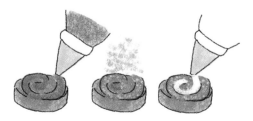

idea

Decorated only with red,
green and white, these
cookies would be a great
Christmas treat.

CANDY CLAY
lollipops

Recipes

- □ candy clay (2 batches, 1 with chocolate chips and 1 with white candy melts) (page 35)

idea

Instead of chocolate, make the second log in the spiral with white candy clay or another color.

Supplies

- □ chocolate chips
- □ white candy melts
- □ oil-based food coloring (blue, pink, orange, purple, yellow and green candy colors)
- □ light corn syrup
- □ lollipop sticks

Techniques

- □ mix color into candy clay
- □ make candy clay decorations
- □ put sweets on sticks

1. Make 2 batches of candy clay, 1 with chocolate chips and 1 with white candy melts. Remember to let the clay set several hours before using.

2. Divide, knead and tint the white candy clay desired colors. Blue, pink, orange, purple, yellow and green used here.

3. For each lollipop, roll 2 logs, 1 chocolate and 1 color. To roll a log, roll a ball of candy clay 1 inch in diameter. Roll the ball to form a log ¼ inch thick and 5½ inches long. Trim the ends of each log so they are the same length. Twist the 2 logs and roll with your palm, continuing to twist and roll until the 2 logs are blended into 1. Roll the log in a spiral and secure the end with a dab of light corn syrup.

4. Carefully insert a lollipop stick at the end of the spiral.

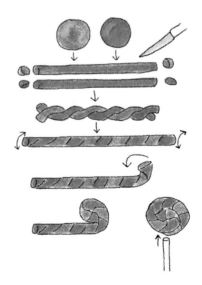

pink princess
CUPCAKES

Recipes

- ☐ fondant (store-bought recommended) (page 32)
- ☐ cupcakes (page 24)
- ☐ buttercream frosting (page 30)

Supplies

- ☐ gel paste food coloring (pink, white)*
- ☐ rolling pin
- ☐ confectioners' sugar
- ☐ 2¼-inch circle cookie or fondant cutter**

Supplies (cont'd)

- ☐ wax paper
- ☐ black edible writer
- ☐ toothpick
- ☐ light corn syrup
- ☐ pink sprinkles
- ☐ cupcake liners
- ☐ decorating bag
- ☐ coupler
- ☐ decorating tip, size 32***
- ☐ rubber band

*Electric Pink and Bright White used here. If using store-bought white fondant, you won't need additional white coloring.

**Use any circle cutter of comparable size.

***Use any preferred size open star tip.

Techniques

- ☐ mix color into fondant
- ☐ make fondant decorations
- ☐ use edible writers
- ☐ use sprinkles and candy
- ☐ mix color into icing and frosting
- ☐ assemble a decorating bag
- ☐ pipe with a decorating bag
- ☐ frost cupcakes

idea

If you're preparing yellow cupcakes, add pink food coloring to the batter before baking to make these pink.

1. Prepare fondant. If necessary, brighten with white food coloring.

2. Roll out white fondant on a surface dusted with confectioners' sugar. Cut out circles and let stiffen a few hours or overnight on a piece of wax paper.

3. **For the wand,** use the edible writer to draw a 5-point star and a stick on a fondant circle. Let dry about 10 minutes. Use the toothpick to dab light corn syrup to fill the star completely. Sprinkle sprinkles over the fondant topper and turn over to remove excess. If there are errant sprinkles, wait until the topper completely dries and brush them off carefully.

For the crown, use a toothpick to make 4 dots with light corn syrup. Sprinkle with sprinkles and turn over to remove excess. Draw the crown with the edible writer as shown.

4. Bake cupcakes in your chosen liners according to the recipe and let cool completely.

5. Prepare buttercream frosting according to the recipe and tint pink. Assemble a decorating bag with the coupler and tip. Fill with the frosting and close tightly with a rubber band.

6. Pipe to frost the cupcake and immediately add pink sprinkles, if desired.

7. Prop the fondant toppers on the cupcakes.

shortcut and tip
Use a larger decorating bag to speed things along.

crazy chocolate
LOLLIPOPS

1. Line a baking tray (or trays for many lollipops) with wax or parchment paper and set aside.

2. Melt chocolate according to the recipe directions. If you melt on the stove top, transfer the melted chocolate to a disposable decorating bag. The easiest method is to melt the chocolate chips right in the disposable decorating bag in the microwave.

3. Twist the decorating bag at the top of the melted chocolate and hold the bag at the twisted part. Snip the corner of the bag ¼ inch. Start piping a chocolate design on the wax paper, pause, lay your lollipop stick on the design, and continue to pipe the design with chocolate, covering the lollipop stick. Pipe as controlled or crazy a pattern as you like.

4. Refrigerate the lollipops until set, several hours. If you are using candy melts, let the lollipops set at room temperature.

sprinkle
MARSHMALLOW POPS

Recipe

- ☐ melting chocolate and candy melts (page 34)

(page 34)

idea

Use four-inch lollipop sticks to make cupcake or cake toppers.

Supplies

- ☐ lollipop sticks
- ☐ marshmallows
- ☐ deep bowl
- ☐ paper towels
- ☐ sprinkles*
- ☐ Styrofoam block
- ☐ candy melts*
- ☐ double boiler or bowl and saucepan or microwave-safe bowl

*Use any desired colors of candy melts and sprinkles.

Techniques

- ☐ dip sweets in candy melts
- ☐ use sprinkles and candy

tip

A funnel comes in handy here, to pour the excess sprinkles back in their container.

The quick version:

1. Insert lollipop sticks into marshmallows.

2. Working with 1 marshmallow at a time, dip a marshmallow in a bowl of water, completely submerging it, and quickly remove. Dab the excess water on a paper towel, hold the marshmallow over an empty bowl or plate, and shake sprinkles over it to completely coat. Prop in a Styrofoam block to dry.

The dipped version:

1. Insert lollipop sticks into marshmallows.

2. Melt candy melts according to the recipe instructions.

3. Working with 1 marshmallow at a time, dip a marshmallow in candy melts, hold it over an empty bowl or plate, and shake sprinkles over the marshmallow to completely coat. Prop in a Styrofoam block to dry.

idea
To display on your dessert table, gather three pops in a bouquet and wrap a rubber band tightly at the center of the sticks. Wrap a small piece of thick ribbon around the rubber band, securing with a piece of double-sided tape.

smiley
COOKIE POPS

Recipes

- ☐ cookies (page 21)
- ☐ royal icing (page 29)

Techniques

- ☐ put sweets on sticks
- ☐ assemble a decorating bag
- ☐ pipe with a decorating bag
- ☐ flood royal icing
- ☐ use edible writers

Supplies

- ☐ 2½-inch circle cookie or fondant cutter*
- ☐ cookie or lollipop sticks
- ☐ gel paste food coloring (black and any assortment of bright colors)**
- ☐ 7 decorating bags
- ☐ coupler
- ☐ decorating tip, size 3
- ☐ rubber bands
- ☐ black edible writer

*Use any size circle up to 3 inches.

**Super Black, Electric Pink, Orange, Egg Yellow, Electric Green, Sky Blue and Electric Purple used here.

shortcut and tip

You may also dip these cookies in candy melts instead of using the royal icing, but note that edible writers don't write quite as well on candy melts.

1. Roll out chilled cookie dough, cut out 2½-inch circles, insert lollipop sticks and bake according to the recipe. Let cool completely.

2. Prepare royal icing according to the recipe, divide and tint black and any other preferred colors. Prepare a decorating bag with a coupler and size 3 tip. Fill the bag with black icing, tie closed tightly with a rubber band, and cover and reserve remaining colors.

3. Pipe black circle outlines on the cookies and let set about 15 minutes.

4. Use the remaining empty decorating bags to flood each of the cookies with brightly colored icing according to the technique instructions. Let the cookies dry overnight.

5. Draw faces on the cookies with the black edible writer.

sporty
PETITS FOURS

Recipes

- ☐ chocolate petits fours (page 26)
- ☐ buttercream frosting (page 30)
- ☐ fondant (store-bought recommended) (page 32)

Techniques

- ☐ mix color into icing and frosting
- ☐ assemble a decorating bag
- ☐ pipe with a decorating bag
- ☐ mix color into fondant
- ☐ make fondant decorations
- ☐ use edible writers

Supplies

- ☐ 1½-inch square cookie or fondant cutter*
- ☐ gel paste food coloring (green, brown and white)**
- ☐ decorating bag
- ☐ coupler
- ☐ decorating tip (multi-opening tip size 233)
- ☐ rubber band
- ☐ rolling pin
- ☐ confectioners' sugar
- ☐ pizza cutter or knife
- ☐ toothpicks
- ☐ light corn syrup
- ☐ black edible writer
- ☐ scissors
- ☐ red paper
- ☐ glue stick

*Use any size square.

**Electric Green, Chocolate Brown and Bright White used here. If using store-bought white fondant, you won't need additional white coloring.

shortcut and tip

Use store-bought brownies and store-bought frosting. Thicken store-bought frosting with confectioners' sugar to ensure you have the right texture when piping the grass.

1. Bake your petits fours according to the recipe and let cool completely. Cut out 1½-inch squares.

2. Prepare buttercream frosting according to the recipe and tint lime green. Assemble a decorating bag with the coupler and tip, fill with frosting and close tightly with a rubber band.

3. If desired, stack petits fours with a layer of frosting, or just use them singly. Pipe lime green frosting on top of petits fours to make grass.

4. Prepare fondant, divide and tint brown (for the footballs) and white (for the other balls and details on the footballs).

5. **To make a football,** roll a 1-inch ball of brown fondant. Pinch and roll the ends to taper, making a football shape. Roll white fondant thinly on a surface dusted with confectioners' sugar. Using the pizza cutter, cut thin strips about ⅛ inch wide and 1½ inches long. Wrap 2 around either end of the football, snipping the ends. With a toothpick, dab light corn syrup on the underside of the strips if needed to adhere. Cut out a thin white strip about ⅛ inch by ⅜ inch and adhere to the top of the football.

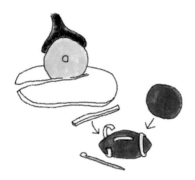

tip

How to draw a soccer ball pattern: Start at the top of your white sphere. Draw and fill a black pentagon. Draw lines extending from each of the five points. At the end of each of those points, draw five more pentagons. Connect each of those five pentagons to each other with lines. Repeat. You'll end up with black pentagons and white hexagons. Or just draw black circles evenly spaced all over the ball, and then connect them with black lines. Don't worry. Once they are sitting on the petit four field, everyone will know they are soccer balls.

To make a soccer ball, roll a 1-inch ball of white fondant. Holding the bottom, draw the design on the soccer ball with the black edible writer, set aside to dry about 15 minutes, and then continue the design on the other side.

To make a golf ball, roll a ball of pea-size fondant. Let stiffen about an hour so it doesn't lose its shape when making the indentations. With a toothpick, poke small indentations all over the ball.

6. Place the balls on the grass-topped petits fours. If desired, cut out a red diamond from paper, glue and fold around the top of a toothpick. Insert into the golfing petit four.

prop
COOKIE POPS

Recipes

- ☐ cookies (page 21)
- ☐ royal icing (page 29)

Supplies

- ☐ mustache, bow tie and eyeglasses cookie cutters (or use the templates)
- ☐ cookie or lollipop sticks
- ☐ gel paste food coloring (brown, black, white, red and blue)*
- ☐ 6 decorating bags

Supplies (cont'd)

- ☐ 3 couplers
- ☐ 4 decorating tips, two size 2, one size 3 and one size 5
- ☐ rubber bands

*Chocolate Brown, Super Black, Bright White, Red Red and Sky Blue used here.

Techniques

- ☐ put sweets on sticks
- ☐ mix color into icing and frosting
- ☐ assemble a decorating bag
- ☐ pipe with a decorating bag
- ☐ flood royal icing

idea

Prop Cookie Pops are perfect for birthday parties featuring photo booths or a spy-themed party. Play around with different shapes. Try different mustaches and beards, cat's-eye glasses, rounded glasses, ties, monocles and so on.

1. Roll out chilled cookie dough, cut out your mustaches, bow ties and eyeglasses with the cookie cutters or templates, insert sticks in the widest part of the cookie (centered to one side) or in the center of the cookie if the stick fits comfortably and bake according to the recipe. Let cool completely.

2. Prepare royal icing according to the recipe, divide and tint. Use any preferred colors for the mustaches (such as brown or gray), bow ties and eyeglass frames. You'll also need black and white. I used black, white, brown, bright blue and red. Prepare 3 decorating bags with couplers and 3 different size tips. Fill the bag with the size 3 tip with the black icing, the bag with the size 5 tip with the brown icing, and the bag with the size 2 tip with half of the white icing. Cover and reserve the rest of the white icing and the blue and red icing for flooding. Close the bags tightly with rubber bands.

3. Outline your eyeglasses, mustaches and bowties with the black icing as shown. Let set about 15 minutes.

4. **For the mustache,** pipe the brown icing to fill the mustache, piping in the direction of the "hair" growth so the lines of icing look like hair. Let dry overnight before handling.

   For the eyeglasses, pipe to fill the frames with brown icing. For the glass area, use an empty decorating bag to flood white icing according to the technique instructions. Let dry several hours; then pipe highlights on top of the white icing with the black icing after switching to a size 2 decorating tip. Let dry overnight before handling.

For the bow ties, use empty decorating bags to flood the bow tie with red or blue icing according to the technique instructions. Let the icing set several hours and pipe dots using the white icing in the decorating bag. Let dry overnight before handling.

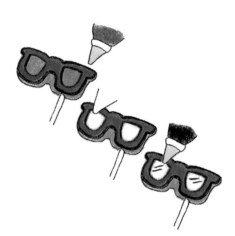

MARSHMALLOW
village

Recipe

- ☐ fondant (store-bought recommended) (page 32)

Techniques

- ☐ mix color into fondant
- ☐ make fondant decorations
- ☐ use edible writers

Supplies

- ☐ 2½-inch circle cookie or fondant cutter
- ☐ pencil
- ☐ cereal box or comparable thin cardboard
- ☐ scissors
- ☐ marshmallows
- ☐ tape
- ☐ gel paste food coloring (black)*

- ☐ rolling pin
- ☐ confectioners' sugar
- ☐ sharp knife
- ☐ light corn syrup
- ☐ wax paper
- ☐ edible writers

*Super Black used here to make the roofs gray, but you may use any preferred color.

1. Using the cookie cutter as a guide, trace a 2½-inch circle on a cereal box or thin cardboard. Cut out the circle. Cut a wedge, a quarter of the circle. Overlap the cut edges of the wedge to make a cone. Test that the roof sits snugly on the marshmallow, and tape the edges securely.

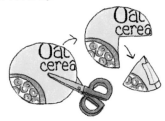

2. Prepare fondant and tint gray with a few drops of black food coloring.

3. Roll fondant thinly, ⅛-inch thick, using confectioners' sugar to prevent sticking. Cut out a circle and make a wedge and overlap the

cut edges to make a cone, just as you did with the template in step 1. Put the fondant cone over the template cone. With your forefinger inside the cardboard cone and your thumb on the outside, pinch the edges of the fondant to seal (dab water or corn syrup if needed) and smooth the cone with your fingers. Gently slide the cardboard cone out and rest the roof on wax paper to dry several hours or overnight.

4. Draw the house facades on the marshmallows with the edible writers. Don't draw all the way to the top of the marshmallows, as the roof will hang over the top edge a bit. Some tips on drawing the facades: Draw the yellow squares for windows first, then the doors and shutters in your preferred colors. Use dots for flowers. Outline the windows, doors and shutters in black last, as black will cover any color. Let the marker colors dry 10 minutes before switching colors.

5. When the roofs have stiffened, dab a ring of corn syrup around the top edge of the marshmallow. Sit the roof on top, seam at the back, and let dry.

milk shake
CAKE POPS

Recipes

- ☐ cake pops (cake and buttercream frosting) (page 25)
- ☐ melting chocolate and candy melts (page 34)
- ☐ fondant (store-bought recommended) (page 32)

> **idea**
> Use store-bought cake mix and frosting.

Supplies

- ☐ chocolate candy melts
- ☐ lollipop sticks
- ☐ Styrofoam block
- ☐ white candy melts
- ☐ white sprinkles
- ☐ gel paste food coloring (red)*
- ☐ scissors
- ☐ red licorice lace
- ☐ paintbrush and palette (optional)

*Red Red used here.

Techniques

- ☐ put sweets on sticks
- ☐ dip sweets in candy melts
- ☐ use sprinkles and candy
- ☐ mix color into fondant
- ☐ make fondant decorations

1. Follow the recipe for cake pops to bake your cake, prepare your cake balls and chill.

2. Working with a few cake balls at a time while the rest chill in the fridge, use your hands to shape the cake balls into logs with flattened ends. Taper the bottom of the log a bit.

3. Melt chocolate candy melts according to the recipe instructions. Dip the tip of your lollipop stick in the candy melts, insert into a chilled cake ball, and dip ball in the candy melts. Stand the cake pop in a Styrofoam block to set well.

4. Melt white candy melts. Working with one cake pop at a time, dip just the top of the cake pop in the white candy melts, hold it over a plate or bowl and generously coat the top with white sprinkles. Prop the cake pop in the Styrofoam block to set.

5. Prepare fondant and tint red.

6. To make the cherry, roll a ball of red fondant and insert a snipped piece of licorice lace.

7. To assemble the milk shakes, use a dab of white melted candy melts to adhere the fondant cherry to the top of the shake. Let set well.

8. If desired, with a paintbrush, mix a drop of red food coloring with a few drops of water on a palette or on a piece of wax paper. Paint stripes on the lollipop stick.

ideas

• Omit the fondant and use any red candy that looks like a cherry.

• Instead of a painted lollipop stick, use a vintage striped straw.

well-dressed
COOKIES

Recipes

- ☐ cookies (page 21)
- ☐ royal icing (page 29)

Supplies

- ☐ clothing cookie cutters or the shirt, dress and pants templates
- ☐ gel paste food coloring (white)*
- ☐ 2 decorating bags
- ☐ coupler

Supplies (cont'd)

- ☐ decorating tip, size 4
- ☐ rubber band
- ☐ pencil
- ☐ edible icing sheets**
- ☐ scissors
- ☐ pastry brush or paintbrush
- ☐ light corn syrup

*Bright White used here.

**Use any fun print. Lucks Edible Image Designer Prints, Serendipity pack, used here.

Techniques

- ☐ mix color into icing and frosting
- ☐ assemble a decorating bag
- ☐ pipe with a decorating bag
- ☐ flood royal icing
- ☐ use edible icing sheets

1. Roll out chilled cookie dough, cut out cookies and bake according to the recipe. Let cool completely.

2. Prepare royal icing according to the recipe and tint white. Prepare a decorating bag with coupler and size 4 decorating tip, fill with half of white icing, and close tightly with a rubber band. Cover and reserve remaining white icing.

3. Pipe an outline on the cookies with white icing, and let set about 15 minutes. Use the remaining empty decorating bag to flood the cookies with white icing according to the technique instructions. Let dry overnight.

4. Trace the clothing cookie cutters or templates on the back of an edible icing sheet and cut out image. Work with one cookie at a time. Brush a thin coat of light corn syrup on the entire surface of the cookie. Carefully peel the edible icing sheet image from the backing and smooth on the cookie.

CANDY CLAY
crayons

Recipes

☐ candy clay (page 35)

Supplies

☐ scissors
☐ wax paper
☐ ruler

Supplies (cont'd)

☐ letter-size colored paper or card stock
☐ marker or pen
☐ white candy melts
☐ oil-based food coloring (red, orange, yellow, green, blue and purple candy colors)
☐ double-sided tape or nontoxic glue stick

Techniques

☐ mix color into candy clay
☐ make candy clay decorations

1. Cut out wax paper rectangles that are 3 inches by 1½ inches, one for each crayon. Cut out colored paper rectangles that are 3⅛ inches by 1¾ inches and draw color names with a marker or pen.

2. Prepare candy clay according to the recipe, using white candy melts.

3. Divide and tint candy clay red, orange, yellow, green, blue and purple.

4. For each crayon, roll a 1-inch ball of candy clay. Roll the ball into a log about ⅜ inch in diameter and a bit over 4 inches long. Use your fingers to pinch a point at one end. Snip the other end so the crayon is 4 inches long. Immediately wrap the crayon while the clay is still sticky. (See step 5.)

5. Arrange the rectangle of wax paper on the counter, place the crayon along 1 long side and roll to wrap the wax paper around the crayon. The wax paper should stick to the candy clay. Roll the colored paper rectangle around the crayon and secure with double-sided tape or glue.

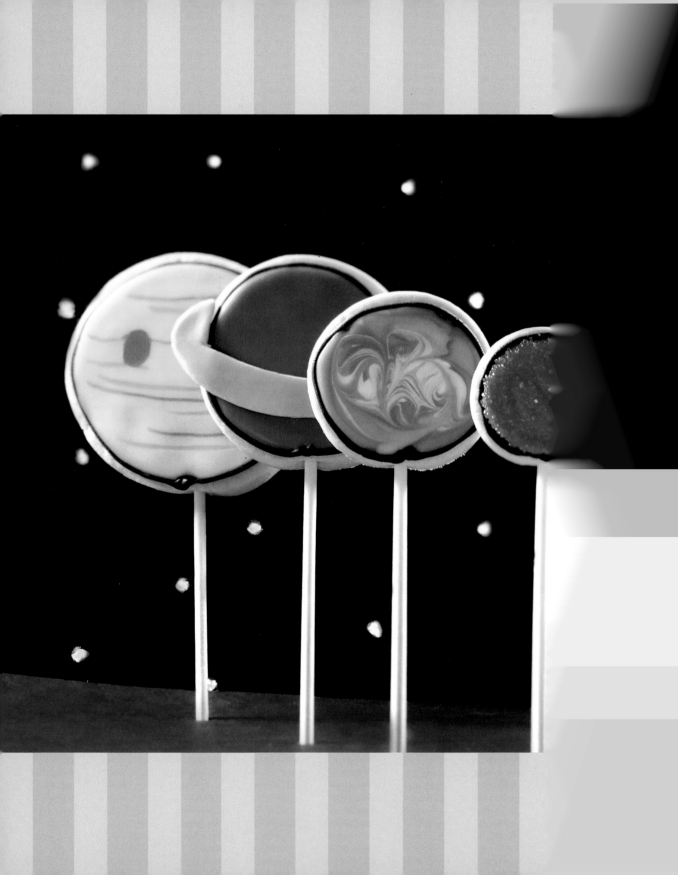

solar system
COOKIE POPS

Recipes

- ☐ cookies (page 21)
- ☐ fondant (store-bought recommended) (page 32)
- ☐ royal icing (page 29)

Supplies

- ☐ 1½-inch circle cookie or fondant cutter*
- ☐ 2¼-inch circle cookie or fondant cutter
- ☐ 2½-inch circle cookie or fondant cutter
- ☐ 3-inch circle cookie or fondant cutter
- ☐ lollipop or cookie sticks
- ☐ gel paste food coloring (black, purple, blue, green, yellow, red and white)**
- ☐ rolling pin

Supplies (cont'd)

- ☐ confectioners' sugar
- ☐ sharp knife
- ☐ ½-inch circle cookie or fondant cutter
- ☐ toothpicks
- ☐ light corn syrup
- ☐ small confetti sprinkles
- ☐ edible writers (black, red, brown and orange)
- ☐ wax paper
- ☐ 8 decorating bags
- ☐ 6 couplers
- ☐ 6 decorating tips (one size 3 and five size 5)
- ☐ rubber bands

*No need to be proportional with planet size. You may also use any preferred size circle(s). You will need the ½-inch circle for the Martian.

**Super Black, Electric Purple, Sky Blue, Electric Green, Egg Yellow, Red Red and Bright White used here.

Techniques

- ☐ put sweets on sticks
- ☐ mix color into icing and frosting
- ☐ mix color into fondant
- ☐ assemble a decorating bag
- ☐ pipe with a decorating bag
- ☐ flood royal icing
- ☐ make fondant decorations
- ☐ use edible writers
- ☐ use sprinkles and candy

1. Roll out chilled cookie dough and cut out circles. I use a 1½-inch circle for Mars, a 2¼-inch circle for Earth, a 2½-inch circle for Saturn and a 3-inch circle for Jupiter. Insert lollipop sticks and bake according to the recipe. Let cool completely.

2. Prepare fondant and tint lime green.

3. You'll need fondant for Saturn's ring and the Martian. Roll out the fondant on a surface dusted with confectioners' sugar. Cut out Saturn's ring as shown, using the 2½-inch circle

cutter as a guide. For the Martian, cut out a ½-inch circle. Use a toothpick to dab light corn syrup on the back of 2 small confetti sprinkles, and adhere to the Martian. Add 2 black dots for eyes with the edible writer. Set aside on wax paper.

4. Prepare royal icing, divide and tint colors. You'll need black, white, lime green, yellow, blue, red and purple. Prepare 6 decorating bags with couplers and tips. Fill a bag with size 3 tip with black and bags with size 5 tips with white, green, blue and red and half of the yellow icing. Cover and reserve the remaining yellow icing and the purple icing. Close bags tightly with rubber bands.

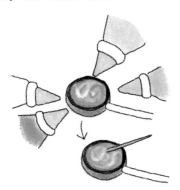

5. Outline all the cookies with the black icing. Let set about 15 minutes.

6. **To decorate Earth,** work with 1 cookie at a time so the icing doesn't set too quickly. Pipe blue, green, yellow and white icing over the cookie. Use blue the most and white the least. Try and cover most of the cookie, but don't pile the icing colors on top of one another. As soon as the cookie is mostly covered, swirl a toothpick around in the icing.

To decorate Jupiter, use an empty decorating bag to flood the cookie with yellow icing according to the technique instructions. Let the icing set very well, preferably overnight. Draw and fill a red circle with the red edible writer. Draw lines with brown and orange edible writers.

To decorate Saturn, use an empty decorating bag to flood the cookie with purple icing. Let set well, preferably overnight. Use corn syrup to adhere the ring to the cookie.

To decorate Mars, working with 1 cookie at a time, pipe to fill the cookie with red icing. Immediately coat with red sprinkles and turn over to remove excess. Use a dab of corn syrup to attach the Martian.

PARTIES
&
OCCASIONS

charming
CAKE POPS

Recipes

- ☐ cake pops (cake and buttercream frosting) (page 25)
- ☐ melting chocolate and candy melts (page 34)

Supplies

- ☐ candy melts (any desired colors)
- ☐ lollipop sticks
- ☐ assorted sprinkles
- ☐ baking tray
- ☐ wax paper
- ☐ drink charms, favors or cupcake or party picks

Techniques

- ☐ put sweets on sticks
- ☐ dip sweets in candy melts
- ☐ use sprinkles and candy

idea

Hit the party store for charms, favors, cupcake toppers and picks or other appropriate small accessories. Use pink candy melts and sprinkles and plastic man charms for a bachelorette party, pastels and baby pacifiers for a baby shower, bright colors and cocktail elephants for a cocktail party, and so on.

important tip

Make sure guests know the charms are not edible!! Avoid or take particular care giving Charming Cake Pops to children.

shortcuts

- Use store-bought cake mix and frosting.
- Use the Sprinkle Marshmallow Pops, quick or dipped versions, in lieu of cake pops.

1. Follow the recipe for cake pops to bake your cake, prepare your cake balls and chill.

2. Melt candy melts according to the recipe instructions. Working with 1 cake pop at a time, dip the tip of your lollipop stick in the candy melts, insert into a chilled cake ball and dip ball in the candy melts. Hold the cake pop over a bowl or plate and sprinkle sprinkles over it to coat completely. Stand the cake pop on a baking tray lined with wax paper. Let the cake pops set, unless you are using cupcake or party picks. If using a pick, insert pick immediately before the cake pop has set.

3. Arrange the drink charms, favors or picks on the lollipop sticks and cake pops. If necessary, dip the bottom of the charm in the melted candy melts to adhere to the cake pop.

cute-as-a-button
CUPCAKES

Recipes

- ☐ fondant (store-bought recommended) (page 32)
- ☐ cupcakes (page 24)
- ☐ buttercream frosting (page 30)

Supplies

- ☐ gel paste food coloring (pink, green, orange and white)*
- ☐ rolling pin
- ☐ confectioners' sugar
- ☐ 1¼-inch circle cookie or fondant cutter

Supplies (cont'd)

- ☐ ½-inch circle fondant cutter
- ☐ coupler
- ☐ toothpicks
- ☐ wax paper
- ☐ cupcake liners
- ☐ 3-inch circle cookie or fondant cutter
- ☐ spatula or knife
- ☐ light corn syrup

*Electric Pink, Electric Green, Orange and Bright White used here. Store-bought white fondant will not need additional white coloring.

Techniques

- ☐ mix color into fondant
- ☐ make fondant decorations
- ☐ cover sweets with fondant

tip

You will need fondant for both topping the cupcakes and preparing the buttons, so make sure to have two batches of homemade or two boxes of store-bought fondant.

1. Prepare fondant, divide and tint an assortment of preferred colors for the buttons. You'll also need a lot of white fondant to top the cupcakes.

2. Roll out fondant on a surface dusted with confectioners' sugar, and cut out 1¼-inch circles for the larger buttons and ½-inch circles for the smaller buttons in your preferred colors. For the larger buttons, center the large end of a coupler on the fondant circle and gently press to make an impression. Poke 4 holes in the center of the circle with the toothpick. For the smaller buttons, just poke the 4 holes in the center of the circle. Set aside on wax paper.

3. Bake cupcakes according to the recipe and let cool completely.

4. Roll out white fondant and cut out 3-inch circles for each cupcake. Frost cupcakes with buttercream frosting using a spatula or knife and top with fondant circles, smoothing edges.

5. Layer buttons in assorted colors and sizes on top of the cupcakes, using a toothpick to dab light corn syrup as needed to adhere.

idea

These buttons can also be used to decorate mini cupcakes, cookies (use the same size circle cutter for the cookies as the buttons) or a cake. To decorate a cake, cover it with fondant, and then use light corn syrup to adhere the buttons.

little lamb
CAKE BALLS

1. Follow the recipe for cake pops to bake your cake, prepare your cake balls and chill.

2. Make 2 black dots for eyes with the edible writer on the Jordan almonds and set aside.

3. Pour coconut on a plate and set aside. Melt candy melts according to the instructions. For each lamb, break 2 pretzel sticks in half so each pretzel piece is about 1¾ inches long. Dip the ends of the 4 pretzel pieces in the melted candy melts; then insert them into the base of a chilled cake ball. For best results, return the cake ball to the freezer for 5 minutes to help set. Holding 2 of the pretzel legs, dip the cake ball in the melts and immediately roll in coconut. Stand the cake ball on the pretzel legs on a piece of wax paper.

4. Use a dab of melted candy melts to adhere the Jordan almond head to the lamb. Let dry.

chocolate letter
POPS

Recipe

- ☐ chocolate candy clay (page 35)

idea

Top cupcakes or a cake with a chocolate pop message. Or, instead of letters, use any fun cookie cutter shape.

Supplies

- ☐ chocolate chips
- ☐ rolling pin
- ☐ wax paper
- ☐ letter cookie cutters
- ☐ lollipop sticks
- ☐ paintbrush or pastry brush
- ☐ light corn syrup
- ☐ assorted sprinkles

Techniques

- ☐ put sweets on sticks
- ☐ make candy clay decorations
- ☐ use sprinkles and candy

1. Prepare chocolate candy clay according to the recipe and let rest for several hours.

2. When the clay is ready, take a small piece and knead until pliable. Roll out the clay ⅜ inch thick between 2 pieces of wax paper. Cut out letters with the cookie cutters.

3. Turn letters over and gently impress lollipop sticks along the back, molding clay back in place if necessary. Refrigerate for 15 minutes if the candy clay becomes soft.

4. Paint the front surface of a letter with light corn syrup. Sprinkle generously with sprinkles and turn over to remove excess. Let dry.

present
PETITS FOURS

Recipes

- ☐ petits fours (page 26)
- ☐ buttercream frosting (page 30)
- ☐ fondant (store-bought recommended) (page 32)

Techniques

- ☐ mix color into icing and frosting
- ☐ mix color into fondant
- ☐ cover sweets with fondant
- ☐ make fondant decorations

Supplies

- ☐ 1½-inch square cookie or fondant cutter*
- ☐ gel paste food coloring (red, yellow, blue and green)**
- ☐ rolling pin
- ☐ confectioners' sugar
- ☐ pizza cutter or sharp knife
- ☐ toothpick
- ☐ light corn syrup
- ☐ scissors

*Use any size cutter for the petits fours you prefer up to 2½ inches, and adjust the fondant decorations to match.

**Use any preferred colors. Red Red, Egg Yellow, Sky Blue and Electric Green used here.

shortcut

Substitute snack cakes or frozen pound cake for the petits fours, and use store-bought frosting. You may not need frosting at all if you use a sticky snack cake.

1. Bake and cut the petits fours according to the recipe and let cool completely.

2. Prepare buttercream frosting according to the recipe. If desired, tint a color to match the fondant. Or leave untinted.

3. Prepare fondant, divide and tint desired colors. Most of the fondant will be used to cover the petits fours, so tint accordingly.

4. If desired, stack 2 petits fours with buttercream frosting between the layers, or just use 1 layer. Lightly frost the petits fours with buttercream frosting. Roll out fondant on a surface dusted with confectioners' sugar, and cover the petits fours according to the technique instructions.

5. For the color ribbon, roll out any color fondant thinly (⅛ inch thick). Cut strips ¼ inch wide with the pizza cutter. Using a toothpick or your finger, dab light corn syrup on

2 strips and attach around a petit four covered with fondant in a contrasting color. The strips should be perpendicular to each other. Snip the ends and tuck them underneath the petit four.

For the bow, cut out a strip ¼ inch wide and 5 inches long. Make a loop, slightly overlapping the edges and pressing together. Cut out another strip ¼ inch wide by 1½ inches long. With the sealed edges of the loop at the underside, use your fingers to gently pinch at the middle of the loop. Wrap the small strip around the pinched center, sealing the edges underneath.

6. Use light corn syrup to attach the bow to the petit four.

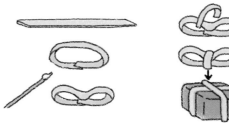

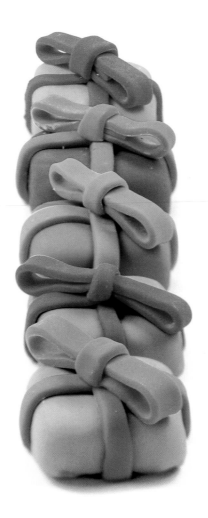

shirt and tie
COOKIES

Recipes

- ☐ cookies (page 21)
- ☐ poured sugar icing (page 30)
- ☐ fondant (store-bought recommended) (page 32)

Supplies

- ☐ 2½-inch square cookie or fondant cutter*
- ☐ gel paste food coloring (red and white)**
- ☐ wire rack
- ☐ baking tray

Supplies (cont'd)

- ☐ parchment paper
- ☐ rolling pin
- ☐ confectioners' sugar
- ☐ ½-inch circle fondant cutter
- ☐ 1½-inch square cookie or fondant cutter
- ☐ knife
- ☐ wax paper
- ☐ toothpick
- ☐ light corn syrup
- ☐ black edible writer

*Use any comparably sized square cutter.

**Red Red and Bright White used here.

Techniques

- ☐ mix color into icing and frosting
- ☐ coat with poured sugar icing
- ☐ mix color into fondant
- ☐ make fondant decorations
- ☐ use edible writers

1. Roll out, cut out and bake 2½-inch square cookies according to the recipe. Let cool completely.

2. Prepare poured sugar icing according to the recipe and tint with Bright White coloring.

3. Place the wire rack on a baking tray lined with parchment paper. Arrange the cookies on the wire rack and coat with poured sugar icing according to the technique instructions. Let dry overnight.

4. Prepare fondant and tint red.

5. Roll out red fondant on a surface dusted with confectioners' sugar. For each shirt, cut out a ½-inch circle and a 1½-inch square. Cut the square with a knife as shown and set the pieces aside on wax paper.

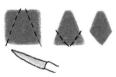

6. Use a toothpick to dab light corn syrup on the underside of the tie pieces and adhere to the cookie. Draw the shirt details with the black edible writer.

wedding
CUPCAKES

Recipes

- ☐ cupcakes (page 24)
- ☐ buttercream frosting (page 30)
- ☐ fondant (store-bought recommended) (page 32)

idea
Personalize the bride and groom by matching the drawing to the real versions' hair color, attire and features, such as a mustache or eyeglasses.

Supplies

- ☐ cupcake liners
- ☐ gel paste food coloring (white)*
- ☐ rolling pin
- ☐ confectioners' sugar
- ☐ 3-inch circle cookie or fondant cutter
- ☐ spatula or knife
- ☐ edible writers (black, yellow, pink, red, green and blue)

*Bright White used here. Store-bought white fondant will not need additional white coloring.

Techniques

- ☐ mix color into icing and frosting
- ☐ mix color into fondant
- ☐ cover sweets with fondant
- ☐ use edible writers

idea
Use these drawings on marshmallows. These would be perfect for a s'mores dessert table at a wedding or wrapped as wedding favors.

1. Bake cupcakes according to the recipe and let cool completely.

2. Prepare buttercream frosting according to the recipe, and if desired, tint white to match the fondant. Or leave untinted.

3. Prepare fondant. If necessary, add white food coloring to brighten.

4. Roll out fondant on a surface dusted with confectioners' sugar, cut out 3-inch circles, spread buttercream frosting on the cupcake with a spatula or knife, top with a fondant circle and smooth with your fingers according to the technique instructions. Let fondant stiffen several hours.

5. Follow the steps below to draw your bouquet, wedding cake and ring with the edible writers.

To draw a bouquet:
1. Draw and fill circles with pink.
2. Draw the band beneath the circles in black.
3. Draw green lines under the band and among the pink circles.
4. Draw red swirls on top of the pink circles.

To draw a wedding cake:

1. Draw a rectangle with rounded edges with black, but don't draw the bottom side.
2. Repeat with 2 larger shapes beneath the first.
3. Draw designs with pink.
4. Draw bride and groom on top, using any desired color to personalize hair, or draw dots for flowers.

To draw a ring:

1. Draw a trapezoid with black.
2. Draw a triangle under the trapezoid with black.
3. Draw 2 lines in the trapezoid and 2 lines in the triangle with black.
4. Draw a ring with black.
5. Fill ring with yellow.
6. Add highlights in the diamond with blue and add sparkle lines with black.

totally edible
BIRTHDAY CAKE

Supplies

☐ gel paste food coloring (yellow, white, red, green and blue)*

☐ confectioners' sugar

☐ ruler or tape measure

☐ knife

☐ toothpick

☐ light corn syrup

☐ wax paper

☐ offset spatula

*You'll need Bright White for the frosting, Egg Yellow for the flames and any other desired colors. Red Red, Electric Green and Sky Blue used here.

Techniques

☐ mix color into icing and frosting

☐ frost cakes

☐ mix color into fondant

☐ make fondant decorations

tip

Because candy clay doesn't dry as stiffly as fondant, I don't recommend making that switch here.

1. Prepare, divide and tint fondant several colors: yellow, white, and any desired colors for candles. If using store-bought white fondant, you won't need additional white coloring to make white fondant.

2. **For each candle,** roll a 1-inch ball of white fondant and a 1-inch ball of a colored fondant. Using confectioners' sugar as needed to prevent sticking, roll each ball on a flat surface with the palm of your hand until you have a log 5 inches long and ¼ inch in diameter. Use your fingers to *lightly* dampen 1 log with water, and twist the 2 logs together. Using confectioners' sugar on the counter and on your hands to prevent sticking, use your palms to roll the twisted log. Keep twisting and rolling until the 2 logs are blended together. The new, combined log will be 8 inches long. Snip the ends and cut the log in half with your knife. Each log will be about 3½ inches.

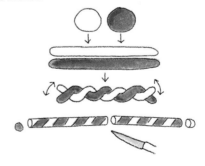

For each flame, roll a pea-sized ball of yellow fondant. Press the fondant gently on a flat surface so one side is flattened. Pinch the top to make a flame shape. Dab the flat side of the flame with water, or use a toothpick to dab on light corn syrup, and attach to the end of a finished, twisted log. Lay the logs with their flames on wax paper and let dry overnight.

3. Bake the cake according to the recipe and let cool completely.

4. Prepare buttercream frosting according to the recipe and tint desired color, including white as an option.

5. Use an offset spatula to frost your cake.

6. Insert candles into the cake as desired.

tip

For extra stability, insert a toothpick at the base of the fondant candle before leaving to dry overnight. This will make inserting the candle in the cake easier. Just don't forget about the toothpicks before eating!

HOLIDAYS & SEASONS

almost midnight
CUPCAKES

Recipes

☐ cupcakes (page 24)

☐ buttercream frosting (page 30)

☐ fondant (store-bought recommended) (page 32)

Supplies

☐ cupcake liners

☐ gel paste food coloring (white)*

☐ rolling pin

☐ confectioners' sugar

☐ 3-inch circle cookie cutter

☐ spatula or knife

☐ black edible writer

*Store-bought white fondant won't need additional white coloring.

Techniques

☐ mix color into icing and frosting

☐ cover sweets with fondant

☐ use edible writers

tip

Because these cupcakes are so simply decorated, use printed or festive cupcake liners to complete the look.

1. Bake cupcakes according to the recipe and let cool completely.

2. Prepare buttercream frosting according to the recipe, and if desired, tint white to match the fondant. Or leave untinted.

3. Prepare fondant. If necessary, add white food coloring to brighten.

4. Roll out fondant on a surface dusted with confectioners' sugar. Cut out 3-inch circles. Spread buttercream frosting on the cupcakes with a spatula or knife and top with fondant circles. Smooth the fondant with your fingers. Let fondant stiffen several hours or overnight.

5. Draw clock faces set to almost midnight on the fondant with a black edible writer.

licorice heart
COOKIE POPS

Supplies

☐ heart cookie cutters*
☐ cookie or lollipop sticks
☐ gel paste food coloring (pink)**
☐ 4 decorating bags
☐ 2 couplers
☐ 2 decorating tips, size 4
☐ rubber bands
☐ red licorice lace or Twizzlers Pull 'n' Peel
☐ toothpick
☐ light corn syrup
☐ scissors

*Use any preferred size, 1½ inches to 3 inches.

**Electric Pink used here.

Techniques

☐ mix color into icing and frosting
☐ assemble a decorating bag
☐ pipe with a decorating bag
☐ flood royal icing
☐ use sprinkles and candy

tip

Lay the licorice on the hearts to plan your design before adding the light corn syrup glue.

idea

Use white food coloring instead of pink.

1. Roll out chilled cookie dough, cut out hearts, insert lollipop sticks and bake according to the recipe. Let cool completely.

2. Prepare royal icing according to the recipe, divide in half and tint 2 shades of pink. Prepare 2 decorating bags with couplers and size 4 decorating tips, fill with half of each shade and close tightly with rubber bands. Cover and reserve remaining pink icing.

3. Pipe an outline on the cookies with either shade of pink, and let set about 15 minutes.

Use the remaining empty decorating bags to flood the cookies with either shade of pink according to the technique instructions. Let dry overnight.

4. Take a piece of red licorice lace or pull off a piece of Twizzlers Pull 'n' Peel. With a toothpick, dab light corn syrup on the licorice to use as glue, and decorate the hearts with stripes, checks or swirls. Snip the excess licorice with scissors. Let the cookies dry well.

conversation heart
CUPCAKES

Recipes

- [ ] fondant (store-bought recommended) (page 32)
- [ ] cupcakes (page 25)
- [ ] buttercream frosting (page 30)

Supplies

- [ ] gel paste food coloring (white, pink, turquoise, purple and green)*
- [ ] rolling pin
- [ ] confectioners' sugar
- [ ] 1½-inch heart cookie or fondant cutter**
- [ ] wax paper

Supplies (cont'd)

- [ ] edible writers***
- [ ] mini letter rubber stamps
- [ ] cupcake liners
- [ ] decorating bag
- [ ] coupler
- [ ] open star tip, size 32****
- [ ] rubber band

*Use any preferred colors. Bright White, Electric Pink, Turquoise, Electric Purple and Electric Green used here.

**Use any comparable size heart cutter.

***Purple, pink and blue edible writers used here.

****Use any size textured tip you prefer.

Techniques

- [ ] mix color into fondant
- [ ] make fondant decorations
- [ ] mix color into icing and frosting
- [ ] assemble a decorating bag
- [ ] pipe with a decorating bag
- [ ] frost cupcakes
- [ ] stamp with food coloring

> **tip**
> Use a large decorating bag to frost the cupcakes more quickly.

1. Prepare fondant, divide and tint desired colors.

2. Roll out fondant on a surface dusted with confectioners' sugar and cut out hearts. Let stiffen on wax paper several hours or overnight.

3. Use preferred colors of edible writers to color rubber stamps and stamp messages on the fondant according to the technique instructions. Set aside on wax paper.

4. Bake cupcakes according to the recipe and let cool completely.

5. Prepare frosting and tint white. Prepare a decorating bag with coupler and tip, fill with frosting and close with a rubber band.

6. Pipe to frost cupcakes according to the technique instructions.

7. Prop the fondant hearts on the cupcakes.

idea
Use this method to make
cookies, too. Just top
heart cookies with fondant
or flooded royal icing.

bunny (and a silly chick)
COOKIE POPS

Recipes

- ☐ cookies (page 21)
- ☐ royal icing (page 29)
- ☐ fondant (store-bought recommended) (page 32)

Supplies

- ☐ 1½-inch circle fondant or cookie cutters*
- ☐ cookie or lollipop sticks
- ☐ gel paste food coloring (white and yellow)**
- ☐ 4 decorating bags

Supplies (cont'd)

- ☐ 2 couplers
- ☐ 2 decorating tips, size 4
- ☐ rubber bands
- ☐ rolling pin
- ☐ confectioners' sugar
- ☐ baking tray
- ☐ wax paper
- ☐ toothpicks
- ☐ light corn syrup
- ☐ edible writers (black, pink and orange)

*Or use any comparably sized circle cutters.

**Bright White and Egg Yellow used here.

Techniques

- ☐ put sweets on sticks
- ☐ mix color into icing and frosting
- ☐ assemble a decorating bag
- ☐ pipe with a decorating bag
- ☐ flood royal icing
- ☐ mix color into fondant
- ☐ make fondant decorations
- ☐ use edible writers

1. Roll out chilled cookie dough, cut out circles, insert sticks, bake cookie pops according to the recipe and let cool completely.

2. Prepare royal icing according to the recipe, divide and tint white and yellow. Prepare 2 decorating bags with couplers and size 4 tips, fill with half of the white and half of the yellow icing and close with a rubber band. Cover the remaining white and yellow icing.

3. Pipe an outline on the cookies (white for bunnies and yellow for chicks) and let set 15 minutes. Use the remaining empty decorating bags to flood cookies with white or yellow according to the technique instructions. Let set very well, preferably overnight.

4. Prepare fondant, and if necessary, tint bright white. Store-bought white fondant won't need additional coloring.

5. Roll out the fondant on a surface dusted with confectioners' sugar to a thickness of ¼ inch. Cut out bunny ears about 1 inch long, with a flat bottom.

6. Lay the cookie pops on a baking tray lined with wax paper. Use a toothpick to dab light corn syrup on the flat ends of the ears and attach to the top of the cookie. Let the cookies lie on the wax paper until dry.

7. Use black, pink and orange edible writers to draw the bunny and chick faces.

idea

Arrange these cookie pops in glasses
or vases filled with jelly beans.

easter egg
PAINTED COOKIES

Recipes

- ☐ cookies (page 22)
- ☐ royal icing (page 29)

Supplies

- ☐ oval cookie cutter*
- ☐ gel paste food coloring (white, pink, yellow, blue and green)**
- ☐ 2 decorating bags

Supplies (cont'd)

- ☐ coupler
- ☐ decorating tip, size 4
- ☐ rubber band
- ☐ palette or wax paper
- ☐ small round paintbrush
- ☐ small liner paintbrush

*Use any preferred size cutters.

**Bright White, Electric Pink, Egg Yellow, Sky Blue and Electric Green used here.

Techniques

- ☐ mix color into icing and frosting
- ☐ assemble a decorating bag
- ☐ pipe with a decorating bag
- ☐ flood royal icing
- ☐ paint with food coloring

1. Bake oval cookies according to the recipe and let cool completely.

2. Prepare royal icing according to the recipe and tint white. Prepare a decorating bag with coupler and size 4 tip, fill with half of the icing and close tightly with a rubber band. Cover and reserve remaining icing.

3. Pipe an outline on the cookies and let set about 15 minutes. Use the remaining empty decorating bag to flood the cookies with white icing according to the technique instructions. Let dry overnight.

4. Mix a drop of any color food coloring with a few drops of water and a few drops of white food coloring (if desired) on the palette. Use your paintbrushes to paint the cookies.

tip

To make dots, use the non-brush end of the paintbrush.

BBQ

MARSHMALLOWS

1. Pull out some marshmallows and edible writers, and draw your designs according to the instructions below. That's it!

To draw mustard and ketchup bottles:

1. Draw a vertical line with yellow.
2. Draw and fill a yellow rectangle under the line.
3. Draw and fill a yellow bulb shape under the rectangle.
4. Draw a red vertical line.
5. Draw and fill a red rectangle under the line.
6. Draw and fill another long red rectangle (note the rectangle is "behind" the mustard a bit).
7. Outline with black.

To draw a watermelon:

1. Draw and fill a red semicircle.
2. Draw a thick semicircle line around the red with light green.
3. Draw wavy lines on the light green with darker green.
4. Outline the semicircle and draw seeds with black.

To draw a glass of lemonade:

1. Draw and fill a trapezoid with yellow.
2. Draw a bent line with red.
3. Outline the glass with black, making sure to draw the glass rim a bit above the top of the lemonade.

To draw a hamburger:

1. Draw and fill a yellow triangle (cheese).
2. Draw a red line on top of the triangle (tomato).
3. Draw and fill a brown oval (going around the cheese) beneath the yellow (burger).
4. Draw a green squiggle beneath the brown (lettuce).
5. Draw and fill brown semicircles on the top and bottom (bun).
6. Outline with black.

To draw ants:

1. For each ant draw and fill 3 black circles. Add 6 black lines for legs.

popsicle
COOKIE POPS

Recipes

☐ cookies (page 21)
☐ royal icing (page 29)

Supplies

☐ Popsicle template
☐ Popsicle sticks
☐ gel paste food coloring (white, green, purple, orange and red)*

Supplies (cont'd)

☐ 9 decorating bags
☐ 5 couplers
☐ 5 decorating tips (one size 3 and four size 4)
☐ rubber bands

*Bright White, Electric Green, Electric Purple, Orange and Red Red used here.

Techniques

☐ put sweets on sticks
☐ mix color into icing and frosting
☐ assemble a decorating bag
☐ pipe with a decorating bag
☐ flood royal icing

1. Roll out chilled cookie dough and cut out Popsicles. Insert Popsicle sticks in lieu of cookie sticks. Bake according to the recipe and let cool completely.

2. Prepare royal icing according to the recipe, divide and tint desired colors. Prepare 5 decorating bags with couplers and tips. Fill the decorating bag with size 3 tip with white. Fill the 4 bags with size 4 tips with half of the green, purple, orange and red. Close bags tightly with rubber bands. Cover and reserve remaining icing.

3. Using any color, pipe an outline on the cookies and let set 15 minutes. Use the remaining empty decorating bags to flood the cookies with icing according to the technique instructions. Let dry very well, preferably overnight.

4. Use the white icing to pipe highlights on the Popsicles.

pumpkin patch
CUPCAKES

Supplies

- □ cupcake liners
- □ chocolate wafer cookies
- □ sealable bag
- □ rolling pin
- □ offset spatula
- □ gel paste food coloring (green and orange)*
- □ whole cloves
- □ toothpick
- □ confectioners' sugar
- □ 1-inch leaf fondant cutter
- □ pizza cutter

*Electric Green and Orange used here.

Techniques

- □ frost cupcakes
- □ mix color into fondant
- □ make fondant decorations

tip

Make a pretzel or fondant stem instead of using cloves for the pumpkins to make these totally edible.

1. Bake cupcakes according to the recipe and let cool completely.

2. Prepare chocolate buttercream frosting according to the recipe.

3. Place chocolate cookies in a sealable bag and use a rolling pin to crush.

4. Use an offset spatula to frost a cupcake and immediately coat the top with crushed cookies.

5. Prepare fondant, divide and tint lime green and orange.

6. **To make pumpkins,** roll a ¾-inch ball of orange fondant. Flatten the top and bottom slightly with your thumb and forefinger. Insert a clove in the top. Press the side of a tooth-pick into the fondant to make indentations.

   To make leaves and vines, roll out fondant on a surface dusted with confectioners' sugar. Cut out leaves with the fondant cutter and set aside. For the vines, roll out green fondant and use the pizza cutter to cut out strips ⅜ inch wide by about 4 inches long. Immediately arrange on the cupcakes.

7. Arrange the pumpkins on the cupcakes. Insert leaves where desired. Loop and twist vines and secure in the frosting.

halloween
GRAVEYARD CAKE

Recipes

- ☐ chocolate cake (page 25)
- ☐ chocolate buttercream frosting (page 31)
- ☐ cookies (page 21)
- ☐ fondant (store-bought recommended) (page 32)
- ☐ melting chocolate and candy melts (page 34)

Supplies

- ☐ about 10 chocolate wafer cookies
- ☐ sealable bag
- ☐ rolling pin or mallet
- ☐ offset spatula
- ☐ gummy worms
- ☐ plastic skeleton (optional)
- ☐ 1½-inch circle fondant or cookie cutter

Supplies (cont'd)

- ☐ tombstone cookie cutter or template
- ☐ lollipop sticks or cookie sticks, cut to 4 inches
- ☐ white candy melts
- ☐ oil-based food coloring (black candy color)
- ☐ Styrofoam block
- ☐ black edible writer
- ☐ gel paste food coloring (white)*
- ☐ confectioners' sugar
- ☐ 4-inch circle cookie cutter
- ☐ scary tree template
- ☐ baking tray
- ☐ wax paper
- ☐ chocolate chips
- ☐ decorating bag
- ☐ scissors

*Bright White used here. If using store-bought white fondant, additional white coloring is not needed.

Techniques

- ☐ frost cakes
- ☐ put sweets on sticks
- ☐ dip sweets in candy melts
- ☐ use edible writers
- ☐ mix color into fondant
- ☐ make fondant decorations
- ☐ pipe with a decorating bag

idea

This cake is not difficult to make, but it is time-consuming. You may also use only bits and pieces of this. For example, make just the ghost cookie pops or the tombstone cookie pops. Or make just cupcakes and top with the chocolate trees.

1. Bake chocolate cake according to the recipe and let cool completely.

2. Prepare chocolate buttercream frosting according to the recipe.

3. Place chocolate wafer cookies in a sealable bag and crush with a rolling pin or mallet.

4. Use the offset spatula to spread a layer of frosting on the top of 1 cake round, layer with

the second round, and top the cake with another layer of frosting. Immediately coat the top with the crushed wafers, pressing gently into the frosting. Leave the sides of the cake unfrosted. Reserve some of the frosting for your ghost cookie pops.

5. See the instructions below to make tombstone and ghost cookie pops, a chocolate tree and a chocolate fence. Insert the tombstone and ghost cookie pops and the chocolate tree into top of cake. Insert the chocolate lines to make a fence around the edge of the cake. Stick gummy worms around the sides of the cake, into the middle layer of frosting. If desired, break off the arms and legs from a plastic skeleton and insert into the cake. Just be sure to remember there are inedible pieces in the cake, and avoid serving the plastic pieces to children!!

Tombstone and Ghost Cookie Pops

1. Prepare cookie dough according to the recipe. Roll out chilled cookie dough ⅜ inch thick. Cut out 1½-inch circles for the ghosts. Cut out tombstones using either a tombstone cookie cutter or the template. Insert 4-inch lollipop or cookie sticks into cookies, and bake according to the recipe. Let cool completely.

Tombstone Cookie Pops:

1. Melt white candy melts according to the instructions and stir in a drop of black candy color to make gray. Dip tombstone cookies in the candy melts, prop in a Styrofoam block and let set.

2. Use the black edible writer to write the epitaph.

Ghost Cookie Pops:

1. Prepare fondant and brighten with white coloring, if needed.

2. Roll out fondant on a surface dusted with confectioners' sugar. Cut out a 4-inch circle for each ghost.

3. Work with 1 cookie at a time. Dab some frosting on the front and top of a cookie with an offset spatula or knife, or use some of the leftover melted candy melts from the tombstones. Drape a fondant circle on top. Gently press into the frosting or candy melts, carefully stretching the fondant as needed to cover the cookie. Prop in a Styrofoam block.

4. Use the edible writer to add eyes and mouths.

Scary Chocolate Tree and Fence:

1. Place the scary tree template on a baking tray. You may want to make 2 or 3 trees in case of breakage. Lay a piece of wax paper over the template on the tray.

2. Melt a cup of chocolate chips according to the instructions. If you use the stove-top method, transfer melted chocolate to a decorating bag. Or, to skip a step, just pour a cup of chocolate chips in a decorating bag and microwave the chips in the bag.

3. Twist the top of the bag closed and hold at the twist. Snip ½ inch from the tip of the bag. Pipe chocolate on the bottom half of the tree template, place a 4-inch lollipop stick on the chocolate, then continue piping, covering the top of the lollipop stick and the rest of the tree template. With the remaining chocolate, pipe lines about 1½ to 2 inches long to fill the rest of the baking tray. Place the tray in the refrigerator and chill until chocolate has set well.

zombie
MARSHMALLOW POPS

Supplies

- marshmallows
- lollipop sticks
- toothpick
- light corn syrup
- large confetti sprinkles
- baking tray
- wax paper
- edible writers (black and red)

Techniques

- put sweets on sticks
- use sprinkles and candy
- use edible writers

1. Skewer the marshmallows with lollipop sticks.

2. Use a toothpick to dab light corn syrup on the back of confetti sprinkles and adhere to a marshmallow. Rest the marshmallow on a baking tray lined with wax paper to dry.

3. Use the edible writers to draw eyes, mouths and blood, or draw Xs in place of eyes or mouths.

fall harvest
PLACE CARD CAKE POPS

Recipes

- ☐ cake pops (cake and buttercream frosting) (page 25)
- ☐ melting candy melts and chocolate (page 34)

idea

Set cake pops on decorative fall leaves as place cards for your Thanksgiving table.

Supplies

- ☐ candy melts (red, yellow and green)
- ☐ 4-inch lollipop sticks
- ☐ baking tray
- ☐ wax paper
- ☐ food coloring (brown and white)*
- ☐ palette or wax paper
- ☐ small paintbrush
- ☐ small liner paintbrush
- ☐ green card stock
- ☐ leaf template
- ☐ scissors

Supplies (cont'd)

- ☐ pen
- ☐ glue stick

*Chocolate Brown and Bright White used here. Food coloring is only for painting the lollipop sticks, so you may use any kind or brand you like.

Techniques

- ☐ put sweets on sticks
- ☐ dip sweets in candy melts

1. Follow the recipe for cake pops to bake your cake, mix your frosting, prepare your cake balls and chill.

2. Melt red, yellow and/or green candy melts according to the instructions. Working with 1 cake pop at a time, dip the tip of your lollipop stick in the candy melts, insert into a chilled cake ball and dip ball in the candy melts. Place, stick up, on a baking tray lined with wax paper. Let set.

3. Mix brown and white food coloring on a palette or piece of wax paper. For the base coat, mix 1 drop of white to 2 drops of brown coloring. Paint the lollipop stick with the base coat and let dry. Mix 2 drops of white to 1 drop of brown. Use the small liner brush to make horizontal lines on the lollipop stick. Let dry.

4. Fold a piece of green card stock. Hold the leaf template against the fold and cut out the leaf (don't cut at the fold). Write a name on 1 side of the leaf. Cover the entire underside of the leaf cutout, including the strip of card stock between the leaves, with glue. Wrap around the lollipop stick and let dry.

hanukkah
MINI CUPCAKES

Recipes

- ☐ fondant (store-bought recommended) (page 32)
- ☐ royal icing (page 29)
- ☐ cupcakes (page 24)
- ☐ buttercream frosting (page 30)

shortcut and tip

To speed up the frosting of the cupcakes, use a larger decorating bag, coupler and tip than the standard twelve-inch bag.

idea

Easily transfer this design to decorated cookies or petits fours.

Supplies

- ☐ gel paste food coloring (blues, white and yellow)*
- ☐ rolling pin
- ☐ confectioners' sugar
- ☐ 1½-inch circle cookie or fondant cutter**
- ☐ wax paper
- ☐ 4 decorating bags
- ☐ 4 couplers
- ☐ 4 decorating tips, three size 2 and one size 32***
- ☐ rubber bands
- ☐ mini cupcake liners
- ☐ Hanukkah sprinkles (optional)

*Sky Blue, Royal Blue, Bright White and Egg Yellow used here.

**Use any comparable size cutter.

***Use any size open star tip that you prefer for the cupcakes.

Techniques

- ☐ mix color into icing and frosting
- ☐ mix color into fondant
- ☐ make fondant decorations
- ☐ assemble a decorating bag
- ☐ pipe with a decorating bag
- ☐ frost cupcakes
- ☐ use sprinkles and candy

tip

Practice piping decorations on a piece of wax or parchment paper first.

1. Prepare fondant and tint light blue.

2. Roll out fondant on a surface dusted with confectioners' sugar and cut out 1½-inch circles. Set aside on wax paper to stiffen several hours or overnight.

3. Prepare royal icing according to the recipe, divide and tint white, royal blue and yellow. Prepare 3 decorating bags with couplers and size 2 tips. Fill with your colors and close tightly with rubber bands.

4. Pipe decorations on top of the fondant circles.

   For the 6-point star, pipe a triangle with white, and then pipe an inverted triangle with royal blue.

   For the menorah, pipe a line with white or royal blue. Pipe and fill a small triangle at the base of the line. Pipe four *U*s.

   For the flames, pipe a dot of yellow, and then pull the decorating tip upward and away to make a point. Let dry.

5. Bake mini cupcakes according to the recipe and let cool completely.

6. Prepare buttercream frosting according to the recipe and tint white. Assemble a decorating bag with coupler and size 32 tip, fill with frosting and close tightly with a rubber band.

7. Pipe to frost the cupcakes, and if desired, immediately sprinkle with Hanukkah sprinkles.

8. Prop fondant circles in the cupcakes.

sparkly stained-glass
ORNAMENT COOKIES

Recipes

☐ cookies (page 21)
☐ royal icing (page 29)

Supplies

☐ hard candies (red, green and blue)
☐ 3 sealable bags
☐ mallet or rolling pin
☐ 3-inch circle cookie or fondant cutter*
☐ 1½-inch circle cookie or fondant cutter
☐ baking tray
☐ parchment paper
☐ lollipop stick or drinking straw

Supplies (cont'd)

☐ gel paste food coloring (red, lime green and blue)**
☐ 3 decorating bags
☐ 3 couplers
☐ 3 decorating tips, size 5
☐ rubber bands
☐ 3 small plates
☐ sprinkles (red, green and blue)
☐ thin ribbon
☐ scissors

*Use any comparable size cutter, or a mix of circles, as long as there is enough room to comfortably make the hanging hole.

**Red Red, Electric Green and Sky Blue used here.

Techniques

☐ mix color into icing and frosting
☐ assemble a decorating bag
☐ pipe with a decorating bag
☐ use sprinkles and candy

tip

Rolling your cookies thinly, ⅛ inch, will allow you to decrease baking time and will prevent burning of the candy.

1. Unwrap and place candies of the same color in a sealable bag. You'll need a bag for red, green and blue candies. Place the bag on a cutting board or towel on the counter and crush the candy with a mallet or rolling pin.

2. Prepare cookie dough according to the recipe, chill and roll out ⅛ inch to ¼ inch thick. Cut out 3-inch circles. Then cut out a 1½-inch circle in the center, or off center for a different look, of each 3-inch cookie. Place on a baking tray lined with parchment paper. Use the lollipop stick to make a hole at the top of each cookie. Wiggle the stick around until the hole is ¼ inch wide.

3. Bake cookies for about 10 minutes. Remove from the oven, and carefully sprinkle well-crushed candy in the 1½-inch-wide circle, completely filling the circle, but don't pile up the candy, or it will bubble over the edges. Take care not to touch the cookies or the hot

shortcut
Omit the stained-glass part
and just make sparkly round
ornaments with or without a
cutout in the center.

tray! Return the tray to the oven and continue baking the cookies another 2 to 3 minutes. The candy will be hot and bubbly, so be sure to let the cookies cool for several hours before moving them from the tray.

4. Prepare royal icing according to the recipe, divide and tint red, lime green and sky blue. Prepare decorating bags with couplers and size 5 tips, fill with the icing and close the bags tightly with rubber bands.

5. Fill the plates with sprinkles, using a separate plate for each color.

6. Work with 1 cookie at a time. Choose an icing color and sprinkles to coordinate with the hard candy color in the cookie. Pipe outlines on the cookie, including around the hole for the ribbon and the hole with the candy. Pipe back and forth to fill the cookie completely. Hold the cookie by the edges, overturn and dip the iced area into the sprinkles. Turn upright and set the cookie on a tray lined with parchment or wax paper and let dry overnight.

7. When the cookies are fully dry, add ribbon.

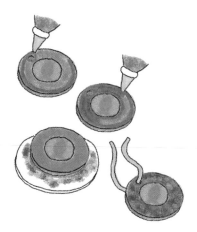

idea

Use all shades of blue with blue candy to make Hanukkah decorations. Or, use a mini Star of David cutter in lieu of cutting a circle in the center of each cookie.

winter wonderland
CAKE

Recipes

- ☐ fondant, 1½ batches (store-bought recommended) (page 32)
- ☐ buttercream frosting (page 30)
- ☐ cake (page 24)

tips

- I make this cake with six-inch round cake pans, but you may use any size cake pans you like.
- Silver dragées are pricey. If you decide not to make this investment, you can easily use white dragées or even large confetti sprinkles.

Supplies

- ☐ gel paste food coloring (white, lime, pink, blue and orange)*
- ☐ ice cream sugar cones
- ☐ serrated knife
- ☐ rolling pin
- ☐ confectioners' sugar
- ☐ cone tree template
- ☐ light corn syrup
- ☐ toothpick
- ☐ silver dragées
- ☐ wax paper
- ☐ edible writer (black and any other colors)
- ☐ whole cloves
- ☐ 6-inch or 9-inch cake pans
- ☐ pastry brush

Supplies (cont'd)

- ☐ white sprinkles

*Bright White, Electric Green, Electric Pink, Sky Blue and Orange used here. Store-bought white fondant won't need additional white coloring.

Techniques

- ☐ mix color into fondant
- ☐ mix color into icing and frosting
- ☐ make fondant decorations
- ☐ cover sweets with fondant
- ☐ use sprinkles and candy
- ☐ use edible writers

1. Prepare fondant. You'll need 1 batch of white to cover your cake. Add white coloring to brighten, if necessary. You'll also need the following colors for decorating: lime green, pink, sky blue and a little bit of orange. Wrap fondant well and set aside.

2. Prepare buttercream frosting according to the recipe and add white coloring, if desired, or leave untinted. Cover and set aside.

3. **To make the trees,** prepare 3-, 4- and 5-inch ice cream cones. A standard cone is 5 inches. To make the 3- and 4-inch cones, place a cone on its side on the counter and gently saw off 1 or 2 inches from the open end with a serrated knife. Roll out lime, pink or blue fondant on a surface dusted with confectioners' sugar. Use the template to cut out the fondant for either a 3-, 4- or 5-inch tree. Spread a bit of frosting or brush the underside of the fondant with light corn syrup. Lay the cone

on its side in the center of the fondant cutout and wrap the cone with the fondant, sealing the edges with your fingers. You'll have a seam of fondant. Use a toothpick to dab a dot of corn syrup on the fondant, and press a dragée onto it. Attach dragées to each cone as desired. If necessary, lay the cones down on wax paper to dry.

To make a snowman, roll 2 balls of white fondant, one about 1 inch in diameter and 1 slightly smaller. If making several snowmen, vary the sizes. Gently flatten the top and bottom of the larger ball and the underside of the smaller ball. Use a toothpick to dab light corn syrup to adhere the smaller ball on top of the larger ball. Pinch a small cone

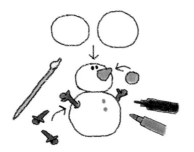

of orange fondant and attach with light corn syrup for the carrot nose. Draw 2 dots for eyes with the edible writer. Make dots in any color for the buttons. Insert cloves for stick arms. Set aside on wax paper to dry.

4. Bake cake in 6-inch or 9-inch cake pans according to the recipe and let cool completely. Because a level top is important with this cake, use a long serrated knife to level the top, brushing off crumbs.

shortcut
Use store-bought cake mix and frosting.

5. Frost and layer your cake rounds and frost the outside of the cake with a thin layer of frosting. Roll out white fondant on a surface dusted with confectioners' sugar, and cover your cake with it according to the technique instructions.

6. Use a pastry brush to brush the top of the cake with a thin layer of light corn syrup. Sprinkle generously with white sprinkles. Arrange ice cream cone trees and snowmen as desired on the cake, using dabs of light corn syrup as needed for glue.

tip
Make pretzel or fondant arms for the snowmen to make them totally edible.

christmas
PETITS FOURS

Recipes

- [ ] petits fours (page 26)
- [ ] buttercream frosting (page 30)
- [ ] fondant (store-bought recommended) (page 32)
- [ ] royal icing (page 29)

Supplies

- [ ] 1½-inch circle cookie or fondant cutter*
- [ ] gel paste food coloring (red, green, lime and white)**
- [ ] rolling pin
- [ ] confectioners' sugar
- [ ] 4 decorating bags
- [ ] 4 couplers
- [ ] 4 decorating tips, size 2
- [ ] rubber bands

*Use any comparable size circle or square cutter. If you are using store-bought snack cakes, you may not need a cutter or the buttercream frosting.

**Red Red, Leaf Green, Electric Green and Bright White used here.

Techniques

- [ ] mix color into icing and frosting
- [ ] mix color into fondant
- [ ] cover sweets with fondant
- [ ] assemble a decorating bag
- [ ] pipe with a decorating bag

shortcuts

- Use store-bought snack cakes or frozen pound cake instead of the petits fours. Store-bought snack cakes, especially Oreo Cakesters, are sticky enough that you won't need the buttercream frosting. Or, if using pound cake or petits fours, use store-bought frosting. You may also use royal icing instead of buttercream frosting.

- Instead of piping designs, adhere a Christmas candy, such as a peppermint, to the top of the petits fours.

1. Bake and cut the petits fours according to the recipe and let cool completely.

2. Prepare buttercream frosting according to the recipe, and tint to match your fondant colors that will cover the petits fours, or leave untinted.

3. Prepare fondant, divide and tint white, red and lime. Store-bought white fondant will not need additional white coloring.

4. If desired, stack 2 petits fours with buttercream frosting between the layers, or just use 1 layer. Frost the petits fours with buttercream frosting. Roll out fondant on a surface dusted with confectioners' sugar, and cover the petits fours with white, red or lime fondant according to the technique instructions.

5. Prepare royal icing, divide and tint red, green, lime and white. Prepare decorating bags with

couplers and size 2 tips. Fill with your colors and close tightly with rubber bands.

6. Pipe any decorations you prefer on top of the petits fours.

   To make a candy cane, pipe a cane shape with red, let set, and then pipe dots with white on top of the red.

   To make holly, pipe the holly's outline with green, let set, pipe to fill the holly and pipe dots with red.

To make a wreath, pipe a "messy" circle with green, let set, and add a bow with red and dots with lime. Or, just pipe dots in contrasting colors.

idea

Easily transfer these designs to decorated cookies. Or cut out fondant circles, pipe your designs, and use these as cupcake toppers.

tip

Practice piping designs on wax or parchment paper first.

PART FOUR

The Techniques

This section is full of tips and techniques that will help you make everything on these pages and well beyond. You'll learn how to put sweets on sticks; mix color into icings, frostings, fondant and candy clay; assemble a decorating bag to pipe icing and frosting; flood royal icing to decorate cookies; frost cakes and cupcakes; coat sweets with poured sugar icing; cover sweets with fondant and make fondant decorations; dip pops in candy melts; work with candy clay; use edible writers; paint and stamp on icing; decorate with candy and sprinkles and use edible icing sheets.

Whew. That's a lot. But don't worry. You don't need to study every single technique right now. Just skim this section to familiarize yourself with the breadth of edible crafting possibilities; then focus on the specifics you need for your individual craft.

how to ...

...Put Sweets on Sticks

Sticks make everything cuter, not to mention more convenient to dip, wrap, serve and eat. I use sticks *a lot* in this book, if you didn't notice. You can make cookie, cake, marshmallow or candy clay pops, or you can pipe melted chocolate and candy melts on lollipop sticks. Find lollipop sticks and cookie sticks in the baking aisle of your craft store in lengths of four, six, eight and twelve inches, though I usually stick with six-inch sticks. Remember, sticks are inserted into cookies before they are baked. And you add sticks to chilled cake balls right before dipping into candy melts, which we'll cover later in this section.

For marshmallow pops, insert a lollipop stick into the flat underside of a marshmallow and push the stick to the center of the marshmallow. You may grease the lollipop stick with vegetable shortening to insert it easily in the marshmallow, a technique that is especially useful when stacking several marshmallows on one stick. For candy clay decorations, carefully insert a lollipop stick into the bottom of the candy clay shape, taking care to make the shape large enough to fit a lollipop stick comfortably, or, for a larger, flat decoration, impress the stick in the back of the shape.

Note that lollipop sticks are different from cookie sticks. Lollipop sticks have a plastic coating and are thinner in diameter, making them easier to insert into sweets, but cookie sticks are oven safe, and so they are best for cookie pops.

...Mix Color into Icing and Frosting

The royal icing, poured sugar icing and buttercream frosting recipes here take coloring very well. As mentioned in the Supplies list, gel paste food coloring works the best. My brand of choice is AmeriColor Soft Gel Pastes, available in specialty stores and online, though the Wilton brand of concentrated pastes, found in the craft store, are good in a pinch. For tips on the best coloring, refer to the Supplies list, and check the Resources section for where to buy.

To mix colors, gently shake your bottle of gel paste coloring and add one drop to the royal icing, poured sugar icing or buttercream frosting. Or if using concentrated pastes, add a drop of coloring with a toothpick. Stir icing or frosting with a spoon to mix well, and continue to add one drop at a time to achieve the desired color. You can make several shades of the same color with fewer or more drops. You can make pastel shades with a combination of a drop or two of coloring and white coloring. Darker colors and white—you *must* add white food coloring to make white icing and frosting—require many drops, but it's best to add the drops slowly. You can always add coloring, but you can't take it away.

tip

You must add white food coloring to make white royal icing, white poured sugar icing or white buttercream frosting. The recipes, as is, are not bright enough. Trust me.

How much icing or frosting should I color?

Refer to the tips below when making your crafts to determine how much icing and frosting you should tint.

• If you are using a variety of colors to decorate cookies, work with about ¾ to 1 cup of royal icing at a time, but adjust the amount as necessary. You will need more of the color you are using for the background, and less of the colors you are using for the details on top of the decorated cookie. A frosting bag should hold no more than ¾ cup of frosting to maintain good piping control.

• For an entire batch of cookies, you will use a little more than half of the royal icing recipe.

• If you are using one color of poured sugar icing to coat a batch of cookies, color the entire recipe. You may even need a second batch.

• To frost a batch of cupcakes or a cake, you will need to color the entire buttercream frosting recipe.

• If you run out of a certain color icing or frosting that you need, no worries. We won't make any crazy colors or combine different frosting colors (like I tend to do on my own), so you should be able to make a second batch that matches the first closely enough.

Color guide. Below is a guide for mixing colors into icing and frosting. This will also come in handy when tinting fondant later, so use this as a reference when choosing your colors throughout this book and for your own projects. These are the colors I use most, based on the AmeriColor Soft Gel Paste names. Other brands of coloring, such as Wilton concentrated pastes or Ateco's Spectrum brand gel pastes, have similar names, and you may choose any comparable coloring. AmeriColor makes about forty colors, so this list is hardly comprehensive, but it's a good place to begin to build your collection. Feel free to mix and match colors or check out the array of other available colors, from avocado to fuchsia to teal. The number of drops depends on how much icing or frosting you are using. Below I provide the approximate number of drops you would use for one cup of frosting or icing, so adjust accordingly.

RED RED. A true red will require many, many drops of red. Lots. This is a tough color to achieve, so be sure to use high-quality gel pastes, such as those by AmeriColor. Too much coloring can produce a bitter-tasting icing, so high-quality coloring will allow you to be efficient with the drops. You may also make a burgundy by adding a few drops of Chocolate Brown to the Red Red, if you don't have the Burgundy coloring.

ORANGE. Use one or two drops for pale orange, a few drops for orange and many drops for dark orange.

EGG YELLOW. I prefer Egg Yellow to the neon-like Lemon Yellow. I use only one or two drops for pale yellow, a few drops for a bright yellow and a few more drops for gold.

LEAF GREEN. For mint green, I use a drop or two of Leaf Green and add some white coloring.

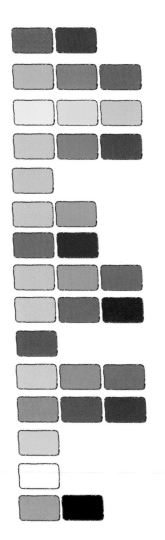

ROYAL BLUE. A true blue requires a few drops, and navy requires many drops.

SKY BLUE. For pale blue, mix in a drop or two, for a bright blue, use a few drops, and for a darker blue, use many drops.

REGAL PURPLE. For lavender, I add a drop or two; for purple, a few drops; and for dark purple, many drops.

ELECTRIC PURPLE. For a bright, true purple, use a few drops.

ELECTRIC PINK. Another one of my best loved colors, Electric Pink is used in every pink I make. Add only one or two drops to make a pale pink and many drops to make a hot pink.

CHOCOLATE BROWN. Use a drop or two for beige, quite a few drops for medium brown and many drops for dark brown. You may add a drop of Egg Yellow to the beige to make a truer brown free of pink tones.

PEACH. I rarely use Peach for anything but Caucasian flesh tone. Use only a drop or two.

BRIGHT WHITE. By far, Bright White is my most used color. You *must* own this, as so many

For a bright green, I use a few drops of Leaf Green, and for dark green, I use many drops.

ELECTRIC GREEN. This is one of my most used colors. Use a few drops to make different shades of lime green. Lime green works well with almost any other color and is extremely versatile.

TURQUOISE. Use a drop or two for a pretty, light turquoise, or several drops for a bright shade.

Beware!!

Though not permanent, food coloring will stain hands. You may wear plastic gloves if you like, or just be aware it may take a day or two for stains to wear off. The food coloring may also stain bowls and kitchenware, so do not use your good china to mix frosting, and be sure to clean up the bowls, other kitchenware and any spilled drops immediately.

Color palettes.
Based on the colors listed above, below is a general guide for choosing colors of icing, frosting and even fondant, which we'll discuss later in this section, when decorating. Feel free to use your own mix of favorites, but these are some of the palettes I stick with most. White and black mix in with any of these palettes.

BRIGHT AND FUN: Electric Pink, Orange, Egg Yellow, Electric Green, Turquoise, Sky Blue and Electric Purple

PASTELS: Mix a few drops of white coloring with a drop or two of Electric Pink, Orange, Egg Yellow, Electric Green, Turquoise, Sky Blue and Regal Purple

UNEXPECTED: Red Red, Turquoise and Egg Yellow

FALL: Burgundy, Red Red, Orange, Egg Yellow and Chocolate Brown

WINTER: Sky Blue, Turquoise, Leaf Green and Bright White

CHRISTMAS: Red Red, Leaf Green, Electric Green and Bright White

HANUKKAH: Royal Blue, Sky Blue and Bright White

designs incorporate white. True white will take many drops, and you must add white food coloring to your icing and frosting to make a true white. You may also need to add this to brighten homemade fondant, especially if you did not use clear vanilla extract, though store-bought white fondant won't need additional coloring.

SUPER BLACK. Super Black is another staple. Use many drops to achieve black and use one or two drops (or a few more) for light gray or gray. You may also add a little white food coloring to a few drops of black to make gray. As with red food coloring, too much black coloring can make your icing bitter, so be sure to use a good brand, such as AmeriColor, to make every drop count.

…Mix Color into Fondant

It's best to start small when mixing color into fondant. Take a handful of prepared fondant, or a ball about two to three inches in diameter. Place one or more drops of soft gel paste or concentrated gel paste food coloring on top. Knead the fondant very well with your hands until fully blended. Add more coloring as needed to achieve the desired color or for darker shades.

If the fondant gets sticky from overhandling, something that can happen in the quest for darker colors, which need many drops of coloring, or if the fondant gives you even the slightest difficulty, let it rest on a piece of wax paper at room temperature, uncovered, for fifteen minutes, or until it's pliable. You may also dust the surface and your hands with confectioners' sugar to combat stickiness.

You will *not* need to add white food coloring to store-bought white rolled fondant or to homemade fondant (rolled or marshmallow) that is made with clear vanilla extract, but you may add white food coloring if you would like to brighten the fondant. If you make homemade fondant with regular vanilla extract, you should add white food coloring.

Store unused fondant at room temperature, wrapped very well in plastic, for several months.

shortcut and tip

Purchase precolored fondant. Because it's easiest to mix color into small batches of fondant, mixing by hand is best when making fondant decorations and details. If you are covering cupcakes and petits fours, you can work with a few at a time, tinting more fondant as needed. But if you are covering a cake or using a lot of one color, I suggest you purchase fondant that is already tinted. Wilton has a limited choice of colors available in the craft store. The Duff brand comes in greater quantities and is also available in the craft store. Satin Ice has the most variety of colors and is found in specialty stores and online. Check the Resources section for more information.

…Mix Color into Candy Clay

You can mix colors into candy clay made with white candy melts. Mixing color into candy clay is just like mixing color into fondant: Knead a few drops of coloring into a small portion of the clay. Add more drops to achieve the desired color. But remember, you *must* use oil-based

How much fondant do I color?

Kneading coloring into fondant can be labor-intensive, so it's best to work with just what you need. Fondant comes in boxes or tubs of twenty-four ounces, two pounds or five pounds. If you're covering a nine-inch round cake, you'll need about twenty ounces of fondant. To cover a batch of cupcakes, you'll need about twenty-four ounces of fondant. Plan on twenty-four ounces to two pounds to cover a batch of petits fours or cookies, but the amount will vary with the sizes of the sweets. If you're making fondant decorations, work with about as much fondant as will fit in your palm, about six ounces, coloring more as needed. Refer back to this guide when you get to the technique "How to Cover Sweets with Fondant."

food coloring, also called candy colors! You can not use the same gel pastes to color candy clay that you used with royal icing, buttercream frosting, poured sugar icing and fondant. So this means you have to buy all different colors for candy clay. You'll find the Wilton brand in basic colors in the craft store, and other brands, such as AmeriColor and Chefmaster, in specialty stores and online. Check the Resources section for more information.

...Assemble a Decorating Bag

I buy decorating bags by the box of a hundred because I use these so frequently. You will use a decorating bag to pipe and flood royal icing on cookies and to top cupcakes with buttercream frosting, and though we do so sparingly in this book, you may pipe textured decorations with buttercream frosting on petits fours and cakes.

You may also use the bags to melt and pipe candy melts and chocolate. Yep. A pantry staple.

I use the Wilton brand twelve-inch disposable decorating bags because they are easy to use, require no laborious washing and are clear, so you can see your colors at a glance. But you may certainly use polyester or washable bags if you prefer, or you may choose larger bags when frosting cupcakes. Couplers are plastic cylinders with rings that hold decorating tips so you may easily change tips on a bag of frosting. Decorating tips help control the flow of icing or frosting when you pipe. Find all these items in the craft store, or check the Resources section for specialty stores and online shops.

To assemble a decorating bag, you will need a decorating bag, a coupler, a decorating tip, a rubber band and, of course, royal icing or buttercream frosting. Open the wide end of a decorating bag. Fold it over to form a cuff. Unscrew the ring from a coupler and insert the coupler into the bag with its small end pushed toward the point of the bag. With scissors, snip the pointed end of the bag about ½ inch. Be sure to snip *below* the edge of the coupler so the coupler fits fully inside the bag. This will help prevent leaks and oozing. Place the decorating tip over the cut end of the bag and hold it to the coupler's edge. Slide the ring over the tip and screw it onto the coupler. Place the bag in a plastic tumbler or a comparable vessel with the cuff over the rim. Fill the bag with up to ¾ cup

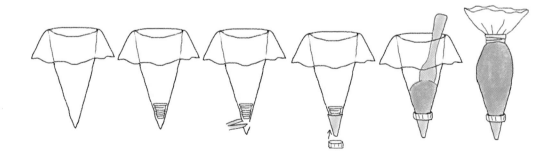

of icing or frosting, unfold the cuff, twist the bag above the frosting, and wrap a rubber band *tightly* around the twisted bag.

Choosing a decorating tip.

The size of the decorating tip you choose determines what you will pipe, so take care in choosing the right size. Follow your craft's instructions when choosing a decorating tip, but here are some general guidelines.

Decorating tips are divided between round and textured. Round tips are best for two-dimensional decorating, such as cookies. Here, we use round tips primarily to pipe royal icing to decorate cookies, though you may also use a larger round tip to pipe frosting on cupcakes. Textured tips, or tips that have ridges, teeth and other manipulations at the opening, are used to pipe three-dimensional decorations, so they are best with a stiffer buttercream frosting and are the standards for decorating designs on cakes. Different tips can be used to make flowers, leaves, stars, ruffles, a basket-weave pattern and so on. Once you get comfortable with piping frosting, there's a whole world of cake decorating scarcely touched in this book that you may want to explore.

For cookie decorating, use plain, round tips, sizes 2, 3, 4 or 5. The smaller the number, the smaller the tip. Size 2 is used only for little details and piping decorations on top of flooded icing backgrounds or on fondant-covered sweets. Size 3 is a good outlining tip and may also be used to pipe details on top of icing or fondant. Size 4 is a good outlining tip for larger or less detailed shapes. Size 5 is used to pipe and fill big spaces of cookie. For topping cupcakes, especially cupcakes with large fondant toppers, such as the Swamp Frog Cupcakes, use larger round tips, sizes 10, 11 or 12.

For a textured, decorative look, pipe buttercream frosting on cupcakes with an open star tip (or a tip with teeth), sizes 20, 21, 22, 32 or 199. You may use any textured tip you prefer,

but those are my favorite go-tos for cupcakes. In this book, we also pipe buttercream frosting with a closed star tip, size 30, or a tip with teeth turned in, for the Hyacinth Cookie Pops. And we will use a multi-opening tip, or a tip with several holes, to pipe "grass" with buttercream frosting.

…Pipe with a Decorating Bag

To "pipe" means to squeeze icing or frosting from a decorating bag in a controlled way. Piping is a vital skill in edible crafting. You will pipe royal icing mostly in cookie decorating, but you can also pipe small designs, such as dots, flowers and swirls, on cake pops, on cupcakes, on cakes, or on petits fours that are topped with fondant or poured sugar icing. You can also pipe stiffer buttercream frosting to top cupcakes and to make designs on cakes. If you've never piped with a decorating bag before, it helps to practice piping first on a piece of wax paper or parchment paper.

To hold a decorating bag, circle the thumb and fingers of your dominant hand around the bag so the frosting sits in your palm, as if you were holding a glass of water. Your dominant hand is the hand you squeeze to pipe the frosting. Keep your thumb and index finger at the top of the decorating bag, by the rubber band, for best control. Rest your other hand on top of your dominant hand. It's important to use two hands to keep the decorating bag steady, even if you squeeze only with your dominant hand.

Squeeze some frosting out of the bag onto a paper towel or piece of wax paper to make sure the tip is not clogged. Unclog the tip with a toothpick, if necessary. Keep your decorating bag at an angle, just like when writing with a pen. To start, come close to the surface, squeeze, raise the tip a little and pipe; don't touch the surface with the decorating tip. Let the decorating bag hover a bit so the frosting falls onto the cookie, cupcake or other sweet. Squeeze with constant, steady pressure to keep your line of icing or frosting consistent. To end, come close to the surface of your sweet, give an extra squeeze and pull the decorating bag away quickly.

To pipe royal icing designs on top of cookies with a flooded background (see below for flooding how-tos), on cake pops that have been dipped in candy melts, or on any sweet coated in poured sugar icing or fondant, make sure your icing or fondant background has set well. Use small, round decorating tips, sizes 2 and 3, to pipe details on top of the icing or fondant.

When decorating cookies that will be coated in sprinkles, such as the Sparkly Stained-Glass Ornament Cookies, you don't need to flood the background of your cookie, because the lines formed by piping will be hidden by a coat of

sprinkles. Simply pipe an outline on your cookie with royal icing, let it set fifteen minutes, then pipe back and forth with a large decorating tip (size 4 or 5) to completely fill the cookie. Pipe in a zigzag motion from top to bottom, leaving no holes or gaps that reveal the cookie beneath. Work with one cookie at a time and immediately coat the cookie with sprinkles and then turn it over to remove the excess.

You'll learn more about how to pipe frosting to top cupcakes later in this section, but you can also use the decorating bag and various tips to create decorations with buttercream frosting. You want a stiffer buttercream frosting, so add enough confectioners' sugar so the frosting holds its shape well, a bit thicker than the recipe in this book.

tips on flooding

• Control your icing. Instead of using an empty decorating bag with a snipped corner, you can fill a decorating bag that is fitted with a coupler and size 3 tip to really control the flow of icing. I skip this step, but if you are new to flooding, this is a good security measure.

• Run out of thinned icing? If you have any thicker icing remaining in the bag you used to outline, remove the tip, squeeze some icing in a bowl, thin with water and refill your bag of flooding icing.

• A word about timing: Unless you are coating cookies with sprinkles, which need wet icing to adhere, you don't need to work with one cookie at a time. If you are decorating a whole tray of cookies, pipe all the outlines first. By the time you are done, the fifteen minutes needed to let the first few outlines set should have passed and you can start flooding your first cookie. To fully ensure your outlines have set, you may also take time out to prepare the thinned frosting before flooding your cookies.

Choose your textured tip, such as the closed star tip, to pipe the "hyacinth flowers" or the multi-opening tip to pipe "grass" on the Sporty Petits Fours. Hold the bag as described above, but keep it vertical to your surface. Squeeze the bag to pipe the frosting and pull up quickly when you are finished.

…Flood Royal Icing

Flooding is a method for decorating cookies that you will use frequently. By piping an outline on the cookie first to act as a "dam," then filling in your cookie's surface with a thinner consistency icing, you will create a beautiful, smooth background. After it dries very well, preferably overnight, flooded royal icing makes an ideal decorating surface for fondant or piped royal icing designs. Or paint, stamp and use edible writers on flooded royal icing that has dried very well.

To flood icing, make about one cup of royal icing in your desired color. You may need more or less depending on how many cookies you are decorating and if you are using a variety of colors, but one cup is a good, manageable amount to work with. Prepare a decorating bag with a coupler and size 4 decorating tip and fill it

with half of your tinted icing. Tie the bag closed tightly with a rubber band. Cover the remaining icing and set it aside. Pipe an outline on your cookie and let it set at least fifteen minutes.

Thin the reserved icing by stirring in *a few drops* of water at a time, about ¼ teaspoon, until the icing is the consistency of thick glue. The icing should pour slowly from the spoon and fold into itself in the bowl so no stiff lines appear; any lines that do form should disappear slowly. The icing should still be viscous. It should *not* be as thin as water. When in doubt, opt for thicker, as too-thin icing is impossible to control and can leave a splotchy appearance when the icing dries. A good way to test the consistency is the ten-second rule. Take a small spoonful of icing and pour it back into the bowl. The lines of icing should slowly sink into the rest of the icing and totally disappear in ten seconds.

Fill an empty decorating bag with your thinned icing and tie it closed tightly with a rubber band. Snip ¼ inch from the tip of the decorating bag. Start by piping an outline just inside your set outline; then loosely pipe frosting back and forth on the cookie. While you want to have icing across the span of the cookie, it isn't necessary to cover the entire cookie; some cookie may show through. Let the icing ooze to fill the whole cookie. If the flooding icing is of the right consistency, you should have to encourage the icing with a toothpick, making sure to cover all the spots and holes so no cookie shows beneath. Let the cookies sit, uncovered, at room temperature to set very well, at least several hours if you will be piping icing only on top or attaching fondant decorations, but I highly recommend letting the cookies dry overnight, especially if you will then use techniques that put pressure on the surface, such as painting or stamping with food coloring or using edible markers.

…Frost Cupcakes

Buttercream frosting doesn't dry completely, so it is not ideal for cookie decorating. Buttercream frosting is best for topping cupcakes and cakes, which are not handled and stacked the same way cookies are. Make sure your cupcakes have cooled completely before frosting. You may use a spatula to spread frosting on cupcakes, or you may pipe frosting onto cupcakes with a decorating bag.

To frost cupcakes with a spatula, spoon a dollop of frosting in the center of the cupcake, and use an offset spatula to spread the frosting out from the center with a circular motion. Avoid touching the cupcake with the spatula, or you might pick up crumbs. You may also clean the spatula, dip it in hot water and smooth the frosting surface, if desired.

To frost cupcakes with a decorating bag, which I find to be much easier and quicker, assemble a decorating bag with a large round tip (sizes 10, 11 or 12) or open star tip (sizes 20, 21, 22, 32 or 199). You can use any textured tip for different effects, but I prefer these tips and sizes. Squeeze a dab of frosting at the center

of the cupcake to build a base so your mound has a conic shape. Pipe in a circular motion to make a spiral. Pipe to the outer edge of the cupcake, then pipe around and around, smaller and smaller, until you get to the top.

...Frost Cakes

If you are making a layer cake from two nine-inch rounds (or two to three six-inch rounds),

first rest the cake on a cake board (if you're using one). Dab some frosting on the cake board first to secure the cake. Spread a good layer of frosting, about ½ cup at least for a nine-inch round, on the top of one round with an offset spatula. Stack the other cake layer, rounded side up, on top. Use your fingers or a serrated knife to brush or scrape off any crumbs or errant cake pieces. If desired, use the serrated knife to carefully cut the dome off the top of the cake to make a flat surface. Then make a crumb coat. Make sure your frosting spreads easily, and if it's too thick, thin it with a little milk. To apply a crumb coat, spoon a couple of large scoops of frosting on the top of the cake. Use an offset spatula to press the mound of frosting down and outward toward the edge of the cake so the frosting hangs over the edge. Then spread that frosting over the sides of the cake. You want to spread a thin layer of frosting over the entire cake, taking care not to touch the cake with the spatula, or you will pick up crumbs. Chill for one hour to overnight in the refrigerator.

Frost the cake with a large offset spatula just as you did the crumb coat. For more perfect results, use a dough scraper to even the frosting and a turn table. Dip a clean offset spatula in hot water, shake off the excess water and smooth the frosting in a continuous movement.

...Coat with Poured Sugar Icing

Poured sugar icing is best for coating cookies, though you may also coat petits fours or pound cake or snack cake substitutes as a tastier alternative to covering with fondant. However, you will see the imperfections of the little cakes through the dried poured sugar icing. If you do coat petits fours with poured sugar icing, I recommend using only one layer, rather than stacking petits fours. Because of the sticky, pulling quality of poured sugar icing, I do *not* recommend dipping sweets on sticks, such as cookie, cake or marshmallow pops, into it.

You do not need a crumb coat for cookies, but if you use poured sugar icing for petits fours, snack cakes or pound cakes, it's best to apply a crumb coat first. To apply a crumb coat, use a knife or small spatula to spread a thin layer of buttercream frosting (homemade or store-bought) on your petit four, pound cake piece or snack cake. Chill the cake in the refrigerator for at least one hour or in the freezer for fifteen minutes.

Set a wire rack on a baking tray lined with parchment paper. Use a small spoon or a decorating bag with ⅜ inch snipped from the end to pour the poured sugar icing generously over each cookie or petit four, coating the top of each sweet to the edges. Let the icing ooze from the top over the confections to completely coat them, pouring more on areas that are missed. Let the icing set for thirty seconds; then use a spoon to move the sweet just a bit on the wire rack. Wait another thirty seconds and repeat. This helps to eliminate the choppy edges where the sweet hits the wire rack.

Periodically scrape the parchment paper beneath to reuse the excess poured sugar icing. Let the sweets sit at room temperature overnight to fully dry before decorating. You may pipe royal icing designs, add fondant decorations, paint and stamp with food coloring, or use edible writers on dried poured sugar icing.

…Cover Sweets with Fondant

While I find buttercream frosting and royal icing taste better than fondant as a coating for sweets, user-friendly fondant's smooth surface is ideal for decorating. You can use it to top cookies, cupcakes, cakes and petits fours. So basically everything but marshmallows.

Briefly knead fondant to make a ball, flatten it with your palm to about a one-inch height and roll it with a rolling pin. You may roll the fondant between two pieces of wax paper or directly on a flat surface. If you are rolling it directly on a flat surface, my preferred method, cover your surface and rolling pin with a dusting of confectioners' sugar to prevent sticking, and continue to move your fondant and add confectioners' sugar as needed. Roll the fondant to ⅛ inch to ¼ inch thick. Refer to the box on page 175, "How much fondant do I color?" to determine how much fondant you'll need to cover cookies, cupcakes, cakes or petits fours. When working with cookies, cupcakes and petits fours, use a little fondant at a time. You don't need to roll out the entire batch at once. Cakes, however, do require you to roll out a significant amount.

Covering cookies with fondant.

To cover cookies, cut out pieces of fondant with the same cookie cutter you used to cut out the cookies. To attach the fondant to the cookie, first either brush the cookie with light corn syrup, using a clean paintbrush or pastry brush, or, my preference, spread a thin layer of royal icing or buttercream frosting on the cookie with a spatula or knife. Lay the fondant cutout on the cookie and press gently, smoothing the surface with your hands.

Covering cupcakes with fondant.

To cover cupcakes, cut out pieces of fondant with a circle cookie cutter roughly the same size as, or a bit larger than, the tops of your cupcakes. For standard cupcakes, this is a three-inch circle. Spread a thin layer of icing or frosting on the cupcake and lay the circle of fondant on top, smoothing with your hands.

Covering petits fours with fondant.

To cover petits fours and store-bought snack cakes (like Little Debbie snack cakes, Hostess cakes or Oreo Cakesters, though I most recommend Oreo Cakesters), roll out your fondant and use either a circle cookie cutter or a knife to cut out the fondant large enough to cover the petits fours or snack cakes, both the top and the sides, with at least ½ inch extra. Snack cakes are usually sticky enough to be wrapped with fondant without a base coat, but for homemade petits fours or petits fours made with pound cake,

> ### tip
> Don't spread the frosting all the way to the edge of the cookie or cupcake before topping with fondant, or the frosting might seep out the sides and not be hidden by the fondant.

spread a thin layer of fruit preserves, royal icing, store-bought frosting or buttercream frosting on the petits fours first so the fondant will stick. This can be messy, since you need to hold the petit four while spreading frosting. Just be sure to thin your frosting to an easy, spreadable consistency. Frost and cover with fondant a few petits fours at a time so the icing or frosting doesn't harden by the time you are done preparing the fondant. Lay a piece of rolled-out fondant on top of a petit four or snack cake and smooth the fondant over the top and sides with your fingers. Trim excess fondant pooled at the base of the petit four or snack cake close to the edge. You needn't cut exactly to the edge. Instead, with your fingers, gently stretch and tuck the edges underneath the petit four or cake. Smooth the fondant and shape the corners with your fingers as needed.

Covering cakes with fondant.

Because I prefer my cake frosted with buttercream, I cover cakes with fondant sparingly. But the smooth surface of fondant is ideal, so here are some tips to covering a cake with fondant. First, rest the cake on a circle cake board that matches the diameter of the cake. Dab a bit of frosting on the cake board first to steady the cake. Apply a crumb coat as instructed in "How

to Frost Cakes," but make it a little thicker. Let the crumb coat set just a bit while you prepare your fondant.

To cover a nine-inch, two-layer round cake, you'll need about twenty ounces of fondant, and about half of that to cover a six-inch, two-layer cake. Knead your fondant first to make it pliable. This will require some muscle. On a surface dusted with confectioners' sugar, roll out the fondant ¼ inch thick, moving it frequently to prevent sticking to the counter. Roll it out in a circle large enough to cover the entire cake. This will require some math. Measure the diameter and the height of the cake. Use this equation:

tip

While some bakers refrigerate cakes covered in fondant, I don't ever put fondant in the refrigerator, because when removed, it can collect moisture and sag. If your cake has fillings that must be refrigerated, you may refrigerate the fondant-covered cake, but don't refrigerate any fondant decorations that will go on top. While fondant-covered cakes may last up to five days at room temperature, I prefer to decorate cakes only one day ahead of serving them.

your cake's diameter plus two times the height plus two inches equals the diameter of your fondant circle. For example, a two-layer, six-inch cake three inches high should need a fourteen-inch circle of fondant.

Fold the fondant over your rolling pin to help you lift it onto the cake, or carefully lift with your hands. Position the fondant evenly on the cake, and smooth the top, but don't let the fondant touch the sides yet. Keep it tented away from the cake. Smooth the fondant around the top edge of the cake, and then slowly against the sides, starting from the top and working your way down. This will take some time. Continue to pull the fondant away from the cake at the bottom as you work to prevent it from folding over and pleating. Once the sides are covered and smooth, cut away the excess fondant pooled at the bottom of the cake, leaving about an inch around the cake. Use your fingers to indent the bottom edge all the way around the cake; then cut along the edge with a sharp knife.

Smooth the cake with your fingers or a fondant smoother. If the fondant tears, wet your fingers with a bit of water, and pinch the fondant at the tear. Then, with dry hands dusted with confectioners' sugar, smooth the surface. Then, um, cover that spot with a decoration.

...Dip Sweets in Candy Melts

Candy melts set pretty well rather quickly, so you can add decorations to sweets coated in candy melts the same day you dip them.

Dipping is the best method for coating with candy melts, so this works well for sweets on sticks, such as cookies, cake pops and marshmallows. I do not recommend using candy melts as a substitute for poured sugar icing on petits fours, for example, because the candy melts do not have a good pouring quality. They tend to sit on top of sweets. Stick with cake pops.

Follow the instructions for melting candy melts in the Recipes section. Don't be afraid to add vegetable shortening to the melted candy melts to be sure they are of a good dipping consistency. It will make your life much easier. Dip the end of a lollipop stick in the candy melts about ½ inch. Insert the stick immediately into a marshmallow or a chilled cake ball. If you are dipping cookies, the stick will be baked in them already. Dip the marshmallow pop, cake pop or cookie pop in the melted candy melts, in and out completely with one motion, rotating only if necessary. Tap the stick gently on the rim of the bowl to remove the excess and insert the pop in a block of Styrofoam to set at room temperature.

If you are coating your sweet with sprinkles, work with one pop at a time and coat them *immediately after you dip a pop*, before the candy melts have a chance to set, so the sprinkles adhere.

If you are not coating the pops with sprinkles, after the candy melts have set, within about fifteen to thirty minutes, you may then decorate with piped royal icing designs, fondant decorations, candies or edible markers. To adhere fondant and candy to set candy melts, use dabs of light corn syrup or dabs of melted candy melts as glue. Using edible writers on candy melts can be tricky because the fats in the candy melts may interact with the water-based food coloring pens. But you can do so sparingly, such as adding two black dots for eyes. Just let the candy melts set well so they are dry and hard to the touch. Use the tips of the pens for best results.

tips on working with fondant

- Keep your hands and work surface free of crumbs when using fondant, especially when using it on cupcakes, cakes, petits fours or snack cakes. Cookies leave the least crumbs, but those other culprits leave a surprising amount in their wake. It takes only one chocolate crumb on a sea of smooth fondant to ruin the look.

- Keep your hands and work surface free of water when using fondant. While you may knead in a few drops of water if the fondant becomes over dry (see below), water makes fondant sticky and more difficult to work with.

- Fondant should be quite pliable and should not stick to your hands. If you overhandle it when kneading in coloring or if you're working with it and it gets sticky, let it sit uncovered at room temperature for fifteen minutes and try again. I also sprinkle my hands and table surface generously with confectioners' sugar when working with fondant to deal with any stickiness.

- Keep fondant covered with plastic wrap as you are working with it to prevent premature drying.

- If fondant does get too dry, wet your hands with water and knead. You can also microwave it for just a *few seconds* to soften. But only a few seconds.

fondant cutters, a pizza cutter, a dough scraper or a sharp knife to cut out shapes. If you need the decoration to be pliable to meld to your sweet, such as topping the Lazy Daisy Cupcakes, then use the cutout shape immediately. If you need a stiffer decoration, such as the flowers in the Pile of Posies Cake, let the fondant decorations sit uncovered for several hours or overnight at room temperature.

Making three-dimensional decorations.

In addition to rolling out the fondant, you can make three-dimensional shapes. Roll small balls of fondant between your palms. To make a log shape, roll the fondant ball on the counter with the palm of your hand. Avoid rolling with your fingers, as that will leave divots in the log rather than making a log of consistent thickness. For cubes, just flatten the sides of a fondant ball with your fingers. Or pinch and roll fondant to make any shape you can imagine, such as ovals, cones, and so on. For best results, let three-dimensional decorations, such as the lawn ornament gnomes and flamingos, sit on wax paper at room temperature, uncovered, to stiffen overnight. Fondant will never fully stiffen inside.

Putting it all together.

Use light corn syrup as glue to adhere pieces of fondant together or to attach a fondant decoration to a fondant-topped sweet, to cookies topped with royal icing, to sweets coated with candy melts or poured sugar icing, or to marshmallows. Use a toothpick or your finger to dab the underside

...Make Fondant Decorations

Fondant has a texture similar to clay, and you can manipulate it in much the same way. Make fondant decorations to top cookies, petits fours and cupcakes, or to decorate cakes.

Rolling and cutting out decorations.

To roll and cut out fondant for decorations, follow the instructions for rolling out fondant in "Tips on covering sweets with fondant." For decorations, I work with a piece about two to three inches in diameter. Roll fondant ⅛ inch to ¼ inch thick on a surface dusted with confectioners' sugar. Use cookie cutters, of the decoration with light corn syrup or water, and then adhere it to the surface. A warning: While corn syrup works wonderfully as glue, use it sparingly! Try and dab just a thin smear. Too much light corn syrup and your fondant pieces will slip and slide before they dry. You will *not* need to use corn syrup when attaching fondant to buttercream frosting, however. Because buttercream frosting never fully dries, the fondant decoration should stick to the frosting if added right away.

...Make Candy Clay Decorations

You may roll and shape candy clay following the same instructions as for fondant. Roll out candy clay with a rolling pin between two pieces of wax paper or on a surface dusted with confectioners' sugar, cut out shapes, or roll logs and make shapes with the clay. While you may use candy clay for small decorations and to make candies, such as the swirly lollipops, remember you can't use candy clay on a large scale to cover sweets.

...Use Edible Writers

Though I'm devoting only a few paragraphs to them, edible writers are one of my most used items and a must-have for edible crafters. Food coloring markers, food decorator pens, edible writers, or gourmet writers... These terms are all interchangeable. Do not confuse edible writers with candy writers. Candy writers come in tubes. You melt the contents with hot water and use them like pens, but they do not have the ease, consistency or ability of markers when it comes to fine detail.

Add details to sweets instantly with edible writers. Use them on any flat, dry surface, such as marshmallows, flooded royal icing that has set overnight, poured sugar icing that has set well and stiffened fondant. You may also use edible writers sparingly on candy clay and sweets dipped in candy melts. You may *not* use them on buttercream frosting, as this frosting never fully hardens.

Use writers exactly as you would a regular marker on paper. To minimize bleeding, let each color dry about ten minutes before switching to a new color. Avoid layering colors, as the bottom color will show through, unless layering is for effect, such as blending colors for flowers. The exception is black, which will go on top of other colors, so if you are outlining a design with black, try and do this step last.

Edible writers are widely available, and you will find some in the baking aisle of the craft store, though the color choices there may be limited. I prefer the set of AmeriColor Gourmet Writers, the FooDoodler fine line set, and the Kopykake Edible Ink Pen set, in that order. The AmeriColor Gourmet Writers have an easy flow, most similar to real markers, and these are my go-to choice, but for very fine detail, the Foo-Doodlers have both a great flow and nice, small tips. I find that the dual end Kopykake writers, while they have the convenience of both fine-line tips and thicker markers, flow less easily and dry more quickly; however, the set comes with two shades of green, including a beautiful lime color, which come in handy. Check the Supplies list for more information and the Resources section for tips on where to buy.

...Paint with Food Coloring

Use a paintbrush and food coloring to paint designs on top of smooth, hardened surfaces, such as marshmallows, flooded royal icing that has set overnight, poured sugar icing that has set well, or stiffened fondant on cookies, cakes, cupcakes and petits fours.

The project and instructions will determine what kind of paintbrush to use, but in general, opt for small brushes. The difference between "round," "flat" and "liner" brushes is shown on the next page. Round brushes paint fine detail and narrow lines. Flat brushes paint greater areas. A liner brush is a very small round brush used for thin lines.

To paint on your prepared surface, pour one drop of food coloring onto a palette. A plastic plate, a clean plastic egg carton, a piece of wax paper or anything comparable works well as a palette. Add three or four drops of water and mix with the non-brush end of your paintbrush. Dip your paintbrush into the food coloring mixture, dab it on a paper towel and paint on your surface. To achieve lighter shades, add more drops of water to the mixture. Adding a few drops of white food coloring and water also gives a good weight and better coverage to your paint, so I almost always do this, even though the look has a pastel quality.

…Stamp with Food Coloring

Rubber stamps, available in the scrapbooking section of the craft store, come in a huge variety of shapes and designs, which allow you to create beautiful sweets easily to match any occasion or holiday. You may stamp on cookies topped with poured sugar icing or flooded royal icing that has set overnight, or on cookies, petits

fours, cakes or cupcakes topped with stiffened fondant.

You may use food coloring diluted with water and a paintbrush to paint on the stamp, following the directions above on painting with food coloring, but I find my method outlined below is much easier and more precise and allows less room for error, such as pools of paint landing on your sweets.

Use an edible writer to color the raised area of the stamp. You may use more than one color on each stamp. Immediately after you color the stamp with the writer, press the stamp onto your dried royal icing, poured sugar icing or fondant. Be sure to press well enough to imprint the design, but don't press firmly enough to smush the icing or fondant. You will likely need to add more color to the stamp with each application. Wash the stamp with warm water as soon as you are finished.

...Use Sprinkles and Candy

Store-bought candies and sprinkles are an invaluable way to quickly and easily add dimension and sparkle to your sweets. Candy can also sometimes be used as a substitute for fondant decorations.

Sprinkles. The craft store has plenty of sprinkles to offer, probably all you will need, but you'll find more in cake-decorating supply stores or online. Cake quins, or flat, shaped sprinkles, are very useful. They come in a multitude of shapes, such as large and small polka dots ("confetti"), flowers, hearts, stars, holiday themes, even animals and snowflakes. The "confetti" sprinkles are shortcuts when decorating. Add a black dot to a white confetti sprinkle with an edible marker and make an instant eye, or use the mini hearts and flower sprinkles for bird beaks or feet. Dragées are small, edible balls that are usually metallic in appearance. Silver and gold are the most popular, but you can also find them in different colors. To adhere these sprinkles to marshmallows, fondant or other icings, apply a dab of light corn syrup with a toothpick. When using light corn syrup to adhere quins and dragées to sweets, the same warning used when working with fondant decorations applies: Use light corn syrup sparingly and apply just a thin smear. Too much syrup and the pieces will slip and slide.

Use sprinkles, edible glitter, sanding sugar or sparkling sugar interchangeably for the most part. Sprinkles tend to be coarser and bigger, edible glitter consists of thin, shiny flakes, and sanding sugar and sparkling sugar—my favorite choices—are very fine. The finer the sprinkle, the more sparkly the result, I think. To use sprinkles on buttercream or royal icing, sprinkle generously immediately after you pipe buttercream frosting or royal icing. To use sprinkles on *flooded* royal icing, let the icing set about ten minutes before sprinkling so your sprinkles don't sink into the thinned icing. To use sprinkles on fondant, paint or dab light corn syrup or water on the area, sprinkle your sprinkles and turn over to remove the excess. If you have stray sprinkles, let the fondant dry for a couple of hours; then brush off the errant sprinkles with a dry paintbrush or pastry brush.

Candy. The candy aisle in the supermarket offers a wealth of decorating tools. With so many sweet options, you can really get creative with how you use store-bought candy. Remember, use light corn syrup (sparingly) as glue to adhere sweets. Some ideas:

TAFFY AND CHEWS. Candies such as Laffy Taffy, Starburst fruit chews, Jolly Rancher Fruit Chews and Tootsie Rolls can be manipulated much like fondant. For small decorations, you can use these as a substitute. Unwrap a candy and microwave it for three to seven seconds. Knead the candy to make balls or other shapes, or place it between two pieces of wax paper and roll it with a rolling pin. Then cut shapes as desired.

LICORICE LACE. Red and black are the easiest to find. Snip with scissors to cut the lace to size.

Adhere it to your confection in patterns, loops or stripes. Twizzlers Pull 'n' Peel works well and is widely available.

GUMDROPS AND JELLY BEANS. Arrange candies in various patterns to make designs. You may also roll large gumdrops on a surface covered with granulated sugar and use small cookie or fondant cutters to make different shapes.

...Use Edible Icing Sheets

Preprinted edible icing sheets create gorgeous confections instantly. Edible icing sheets are usually letter-size sheets of paper holding strips of edible paper (meant for cakes, but you may use them for any size sweet), or you'll find sheets with cupcake-size circles. There are many design options available, and some companies will print a custom design to match your party or wedding decor. You will find some edible icing sheets in the baking aisle of the craft store and much more variety online. Find suppliers in the Resources section.

Use edible icing sheets on buttercream frosting, royal icing, fondant or marshmallows. You'll find detailed instructions on the package, but generally, you peel the icing sheet from the backing and place it on your prepared surface, smoothing with your fingers. To prepare a buttercream frosting surface, frost your cake or cupcake as flatly and smoothly as possible. For dried surfaces, such as hardened royal icing, fondant or marshmallows, use a paintbrush or pastry brush to brush the surface with light corn syrup before applying the icing sheet. You may also cut the icing sheet before you peel away the backing to conform to the size of your surface.

...Tint Coconut

Shredded coconut adds interest to decorated cakes and cupcakes, and the texture of coconut can mimic snow or grass. To tint coconut, place it in a sealed plastic bag with one to two drops of food coloring, and shake well. Add more food coloring for a darker shade. Use tinted coconut immediately after frosting a cake or cupcake by gently pressing a generous amount on the frosting.

PART FIVE

The Wrapping

The treats in this book are meant to be crafted for fun, but they are also meant to be served and given.

There's a good chance you'll use edible crafts at parties and events and you'll give them as gifts. This section offers tips and techniques for presenting and wrapping your sweets.

Crafty sweets fit just about anywhere. Use them for...

DESSERT TABLES. Edible crafts should be staples of the popular themed dessert tables, as you can match any theme. For example, use the Fairy Woodland Petits Fours and Toadstool Marshmallows for a fairy party or the Solar System Cookie Pops for a space party. Animal Print Cookie Pops are an excellent addition for a jungle theme, Farm Animal Snack Cakes are perfect for a farm party, and so on. Display Decorative Marshmallow Pops at a more sophisticated soiree, and Charming Cake Pops at a bachelorette or cocktail party (eat a cake pop and add the charm to your drink).

SUBSTITUTE GIFTS. Getting tickets to the Super Bowl? Give them Sporty Petits Fours as a clue. Heading to the beach? Prepare Under the Sea Cupcakes.

HOST AND HOSTESS GIFTS. Bring sweets to a party or dress up gifts with sweets. Dangle a sparkly cookie ornament from a bottle of wine for the host of a Christmas party. Bring a platter filled with painted petits fours or stamped cookies to an event. Or bring a mason jar of BBQ Marshmallows to a summer shindig.

THE GIFT ITSELF. Dad tired of the same old tie every year? How about a box full of the edible versions? Or give a bouquet of Licorice Heart Cookie Pops to your sweetie.

JUST FOR FUN. Tuck the Smiley Face Cookie Pops in a lunch box for a sweet surprise. Or make Crazy Chocolate Lollipops on a rainy day.

PARTY FAVORS. Wrap individual sweets in cellophane bags or little boxes, and give guests treats that match the theme of your party. For example, make Candy Clay Lollipops for a sweets-themed party, or boxes of Candy Clay Crayons for a back-to-school event.

PLACE CARDS. Sweets on sticks make great place cards. Attach a name tag with a table number to the sticks and display them as an arrangement at the door as guests enter.

AS A PARTY ACTIVITY. Have a grown-up edible crafting party, or use edible crafts as a kids' party activity. Let kids decorate cookies, or set up Smiley Cookie Pops already decorated (minus the smileys) and have kids add their own faces. The best inexpensive, quick party activity entails placing a bag of marshmallows and edible writers on the table.

- Treats should be totally dry before wrapping. Ideally, they should dry overnight before packaging.

- Because buttercream frosting won't dry stiffly enough to handle without smushing, it's best to package cupcakes and cakes topped with buttercream frosting in bakery boxes, and to serve them on cake or cupcake stands or on platters.

- Any treat, even those that have dried overnight, can leave a residue on packaging, so never package the treats in tissue paper or other paper products, such as boxes, without wax paper or cellophane as a barrier.

how to package sweets...

...In Cellophane Bags

Find cellophane favor bags in a variety of sizes in the craft store, or check the Resources section for ordering them in bulk for large events. The small (four inches wide by six inches long) and larger bags (four inches wide by nine inches long) are the only two sizes I need. Wrap decorated cookies (on or off a stick), marshmallows (on or off a stick), petits fours, cake pops and candy clay as favors. Place the sweet in the bag, or slide the bag over the sweet if it is on a stick, and tie closed with ribbon.

...In DIY Packaging

Craft your own packaging, such as paper cones or fabric sacks. To make paper cones, cut out the template provided. Trace it on decorative card stock, cut it out and fold at the flap. Roll the cone and secure the flap with double-sided tape. Fill a four-inch-by-nine-inch cellophane bag with small treats, such as bite-size cookies or decorated marshmallows, insert it snugly in the cone, securing it with a piece of double-sided tape if needed, and tie the bag closed with ribbon.

To make a fabric sack, wrap sweets, such as small cookies, a petit four or marshmallows, in a cello bag, cut out a circle of fabric with pinking shears large enough to accommodate your sweets, place the cello bag of sweets at the center of the fabric, gather the edges and tie with a ribbon.

...In Containers

Fill mason jars with mini cookies, marshmallows or candy clay and top with fabric, ribbon, stickers and tags. Find jars in craft stores, hardware stores and supermarkets. Bakery boxes with colorful twine or ribbon make great packaging for take-home favors or sweet gifts. Check the Resources section for tips on where to buy. Or, to display cookies, marshmallows, candy clay and cake balls on a dessert table, use candy and cookie jars in assorted sizes.

...On Plates and Platters

Serve cookies, petits fours, cupcakes and even upside-down marshmallow and cake pops on decorative platters. To give these treats as a gift, set the platter on a large piece of cellophane, gather the cellophane at the top of the platter, above the sweets, and tie it with a ribbon.

...As Arrangements

To make arrangements of cookie, marshmallow and cake pops, follow the instructions below.

YOU WILL NEED:

- Styrofoam block
- Cookie, marshmallow or cake pops, or any treats on sticks
- Lollipop stick
- Wax paper or other see-through paper
- Pen or marker
- Tissue paper or decorative paper
- Adhesive tape
- Needle
- Keepsake container (optional)

Poke holes in the Styrofoam block first with a lollipop stick where you want to arrange your pops. You will need an inch of space between each pop, so the holes will be about two or three inches apart, depending on the size of your sweet. Lay a piece of wax paper or other see-through paper the size of the Styrofoam block on top of the block and mark the locations of the holes with a pen. If you are unable to see the holes through the paper, mark the holes with a marker on the Styrofoam. Wrap the Styrofoam with tissue paper or decorative paper, securing the paper on the underside with tape. Lay your wax paper template over the wrapped Styrofoam block, and use a needle to poke holes. Insert your pops.

Alternatively, instead of wrapping with tissue paper or decorative paper, after you create the holes with the lollipop stick, insert the Styrofoam block securely into your keepsake container, arrange your pops, then add tufts of tissue paper between the sticks to hide the Styrofoam block.

more embellishments

Crafty people like you always have to go that extra step. Here are some ideas for nonedible embellishments.

Add tags

Use a circle punch or other shape to cut out tags from card stock. Punch a hole in the top and bottom and slide the tag on your cookie, cake or marshmallow pop stick. Or, use a ribbon to attach the tag.

Wrap cupcakes

Make your own cupcake wrappers from decorative papers with the template provided in Part Six. Cut out the cupcake wrapper, fold the flap, roll and secure the flap with double-sided tape.

Decorate your sticks

Use food coloring and a paintbrush to paint lollipop sticks to match the attached sweets. If the plastic-coated lollipop sticks resist the food coloring, mix the coloring with a few drops of white food coloring. The white adds weight to the coloring. Paint your lollipop stick with the mixture and let it dry. If desired, paint stripes on top in a contrasting color of food coloring. (The top coat doesn't need to be mixed with white food coloring.)

structuring your time

Crafting sweets is fun, but it can be time-consuming and tough to fit in a day, especially if you are planning a party and have plenty of other tasks. Luckily, most sweets *should* be prepared at least a day before an event so they have time to dry. Other crafts *need* to be prepared two days in advance so they have time to dry overnight between steps. For example, cookies flooded with icing or some fondant decorations must dry overnight. All this drying time, while not very helpful to the procrastinator (believe me, I understand), is very useful for the planner, because you can have sweets ready before your party.

For even longer-range planning, here are some things you can prepare several days in advance.

- Prepare royal icing, tint your colors, and assemble and fill decorating bags. (Don't, however, thin the icing for the flooding method until you are actually flooding.)
- Prepare fondant, tint your colors and wrap well.
- Prepare candy clay, color and wrap well.
- Prepare cookie dough and keep wrapped well in the fridge for up to several days. (Do not prepare cake or petit four batter in advance, though.) Find more tips on making cookies ahead in the Recipes section.

PART SIX

Resources

and Templates

RESOURCES

You'll find most of the supplies you need in the supermarket or in the baking aisle of the craft store. If you have any specialty cake decorating stores in your area, you will be almost completely covered. Some specialty chain stores, such as Williams-Sonoma and Sur La Table, also have a lot of supplies unavailable in craft stores. And you can find everything you need online.

Craft stores

Find many items in the baking aisle of the craft store, including meringue powder, fondant, candy melts, lollipop and cookie sticks, candy colors, cupcake liners, decorating bags, couplers, tips, sprinkles, rubber stamps and paintbrushes. You'll also find fondant, some cookie and fondant cutters, gel paste food coloring, and edible pens, though for greater variety and different brand choices, you will need to look elsewhere. But your first stop should be the baking aisle of the craft store.

FOR LOCATIONS:

A.C. Moore, www.acmoore.com
Hobby Lobby, www.hobbylobby.com
Jo-Ann Fabric and Craft Stores, www.joann.com
Michaels, www.michaels.com

Specialty chain stores

These stores carry bakeware, cupcake liners, cookie cutters, spatulas, mixing bowls, measuring equipment, rolling pins and rolling pin guide rings, meringue powder, and other ingredients, and some of your decorating supplies. Sur La Table carries Satin Ice, a high-quality fondant.

FOR LOCATIONS:

Sur La Table, www.surlatable.com
Williams-Sonoma, www.williams-sonoma.com

Cake and cookie decorating stores

(ONE-STOP ONLINE SHOPS)

These resources may be your one-stop shops. Most carry all the hard-to-find decorating supplies, such as extracts; meringue powder; glycerin; gel pastes and oil-based food coloring; candy melts; edible pens; edible icing sheets; cookie and fondant cutters; various brands of fondant; sprinkles and dragées; lollipop and cookie sticks; and decorating bags, couplers and tips. Some of the shops listed below ship internationally.

Cake Art, www.cakeart.com

Candyland Crafts, www.candylandcrafts.com

Confectionery House, www.confectioneryhouse.com

Country Kitchen SweetArt, www.countrykitchensa.com

Kitchen Krafts, www.kitchenkrafts.com

N.Y. Cake, www.nycake.com

Sugarcraft, www.sugarcraft.com

Brand-name stores

Since you can find all these brands at both the craft store and the one-stop shops, I rarely order directly from the manufacturer, but here are some sites for the specific brands of decorating supplies mentioned in this book. Wilton is the brand found in most craft stores. Ateco also makes great supplies used by professionals. You can shop on both of their sites. CK Products, a wholesaler, offers many decorating supplies. Find information on their products and links to retailers on their site. Make 'n Mold offers candy melts as well as other decorating supplies, and you may shop on their site. AmeriColor,

Kopykake and Chefmaster offer food coloring and edible pens. You may shop on the latter two sites, and AmeriColor, a wholesaler, has links to retailers on their site. Satin Fine Foods provide information on their fondant products and links to distributors on their site.

AmeriColor, www.americolorcorp.com (for soft gel pastes, oil-based food coloring and Gourmet Writer Food Decorating pens)

Ateco, www.atecousa.com (for meringue powder, decorating tips and bags, cookie cutters, Spectrum food coloring and more)

Chefmaster, www.bkcompany.com

CK Products, www.ckproducts.com

Kopykake, www.kopykake.com (for edible ink pens)

Make 'n Mold, www.makenmold.com (candy melts and some decorating supplies)

Satin Fine Foods, www.satinfinefoods.com (for Satin Ice rolled fondant)

Wilton, www.wilton.com (for everything)

Specialty online stores

For edible icing sheets, cupcake liners, baker's twine, bakery boxes, cupcake toppers and picks, and other clever packaging and cake and cookie decorating ideas, check out these specialty shops. These shops also offer many of the decorating supplies you will need, including cookie cutters.

Bake It Pretty, www.bakeitpretty.com

Fancy Flours, www.fancyflours.com

Layer Cake Shop, www.layercakeshop.com

Sweet! Baking and Candy Making Supply, www.sweetbakingsupply.com

Cookie cutter shops

You may find the cutters you need in the craft store or the one-stop shops, but here are good sources for cookie cutters, especially for the special shapes used in this book, such as the eyeglasses, mustache and flowers.

Ann Clark, Ltd., www.annclark.com

The Cookie Cutter Shop, www.thecookiecuttershop.com

CopperGifts.com, www.coppergifts.com

H. O. Foose Tinsmithing Co., www.foosecookiecutters.com

Off the Beaten Path, www.cookiecutter.com

Bakeware

While department stores and the specialty chain stores also offer many options, here are more good sources for quality bakeware.

Bridge Kitchenware, www.bridgekitchenware.com

Chef Tools, www.cheftools.com

Edible icing sheets

Duff Goldman by Gartner Studios offers "cake tattoos," which can also be found at Michaels craft store. They also carry sprinkles, bakeware and fondant. Several of the one-stop shops carry edible images, such as Country Kitchen SweetArt and Sugarcraft. Ticings specializes in edible icing sheets and offers custom orders. Or, check out Kopykake for special printers, papers and edible inks to make your own!

Country Kitchen SweetArt, www.countrykitchensa.com

Duff, www.duff.com

Kopykake, www.kopykake.com

Sugarcraft, www.sugarcraft.com

Ticings, www.ticings.com

Candy

Find inspiration at these sites to decorate your sweets with interesting candy.

Candy Direct, www.candydirect.com

Candy Warehouse, www.candywarehouse.com

Boxes and bags

Check out these shops to purchase boxes and bags in bulk if you are wrapping a lot of sweets for a big event.

ClearBags, www.clearbags.com

Nashville Wraps, www.nashvillewraps.com

U.S. Box, www.usbox.com

Stamping and paper

While the scrapbooking section of the craft store offers many options for stamping, here are some further resources for stamping icing and fondant. You'll also find decorative paper, tags and other embellishments at these shops.

Hero Arts, www.heroarts.com

Impress, www.impressrubberstamps.com

Paper Source, www.paper-source.com

Stampin' Up! www.stampinup.com

TEMPLATES

Find templates here to cut out for some of the cookies, fondant and paper embellishments in this book. Included are cookie templates for the stick cookies: the Prop Cookie Pops, Well-Dressed Cookies, Popsicle Cookie Pops and tombstone cookies for the Halloween Graveyard Cake; a template to pipe the scary chocolate tree for the Halloween Graveyard Cake; a template to cut the fondant for the Winter Wonderland Cake tree cones; and templates to cut out the paper flower for the Flower Cake Pops and leaves for the Flower Cake Pops and Fall Harvest Place Card Cake Pops. You'll also find packaging templates to make paper cones and cupcake wrappers.

Instructions

To make templates, trace the template on parchment or wax paper, or scan and print, or use a photocopier. Cut out the traced or copied template, place it on a piece of card stock or heavy-weight paper, outline it with a pencil, and cut out the shape.

To cut out cookies, lay the card-stock template on your chilled, rolled-out cookie dough, cut around the shape with a sharp knife and smooth the sides with your fingers. Bake the cookies according to the recipe.

To cut out fondant, lay the template on rolled-out fondant, cut out the shapes with a sharp knife and smooth the sides with your fingers.

For the Flower Cake Pops, lay the parchment paper template on the underside of decorative paper, outline and cut out the shape. For the leaves, fold green or decorative paper, hold the flat side of the template against the fold, and cut out the shape. Don't cut at the fold. When you unfold the leaf, you'll have two leaves and a band of paper in between. Cut out the paper cones and cupcake wrappers following the same instructions as for the flowers. Fold the flaps at the line indicated and cover the whole length of the flap with a piece of double-sided tape. Roll the cone or wrapper and secure at the tape.

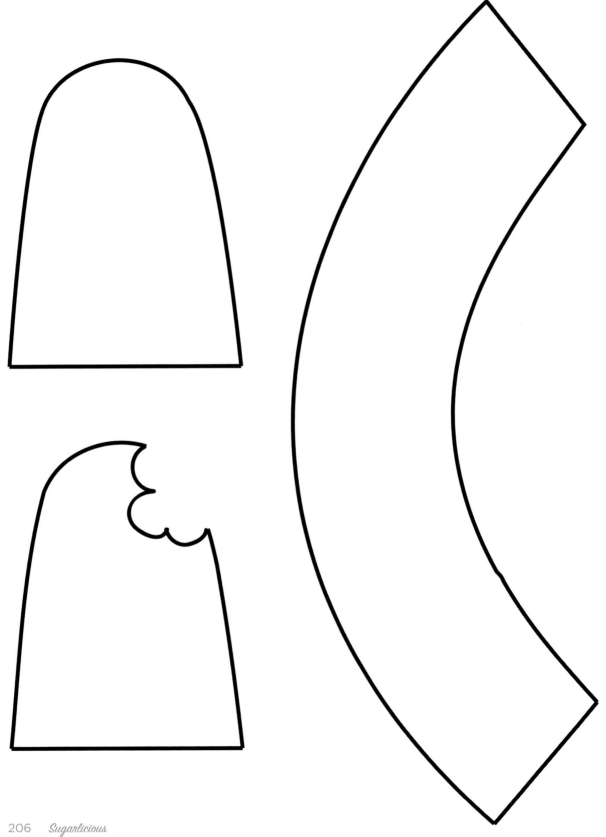

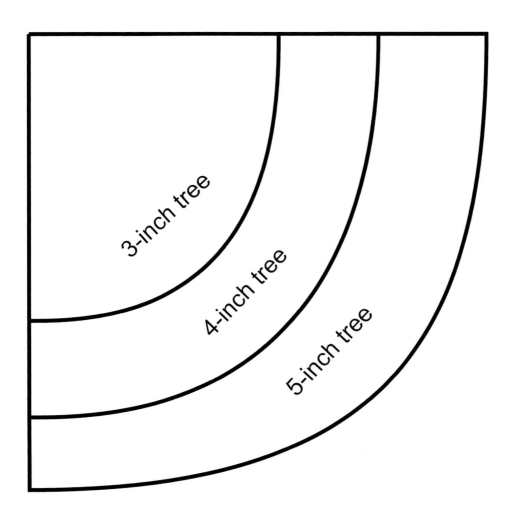

3-inch tree

4-inch tree

5-inch tree

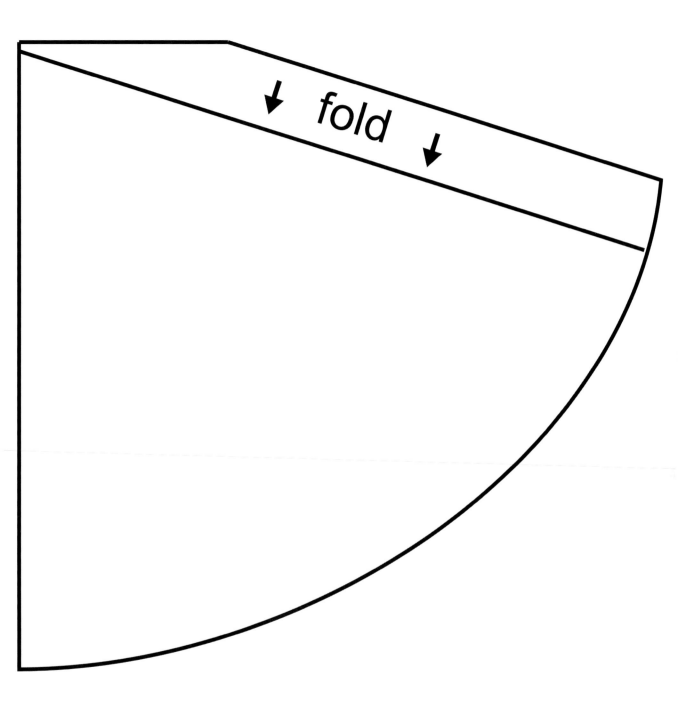

fold

fold

FAREWELL

When I picked up my first bag of frosting to decorate cookies back in 1998, I thought the job would last a few weeks. I had no idea sweet things would consume me for so many years. And over the last decade, I've watched as cookie, cupcake and cake decorating have moved from the realm of professionals into the home kitchen, with greater and greater accessibility to fun, user-friendly decorating supplies and tools.

The world of crafting sweets is so huge, this book should merely get you started. So many of the techniques and decorations here may be mixed and matched and applied to even more goodies, such as rice cereal treats, brownies and beyond. You may certainly find different tools, techniques and methods to do things, too. I'm finding and trying new techniques and methods almost every day. But I hope you now have a solid base of knowledge to give you total control over that baking aisle in the craft store, nay, even a cake decorating supply store, so you can find inspiration in all those tubs and tubes we haven't even gotten to yet.

Be sure to find me at www.thedecoratedcookieblog.com and ediblecrafts.craftgossip.com for more ideas such as those found here, and to share with me your own creations. Happy and sweet crafting!

SUGARLICIOUS CHART

With the exception of candy clay, which can be used all alone, most crafted sweets have three components: the basic confection, the coating and the decorations. You'll find tips in this book on how to mix and match the three components and which work best together.

crafting sweets...easy as 1, 2, 3

1. The Basic Confection
START WITH...

cookies or cookie pops
cupcakes
cakes
cake pops
petits fours
marshmallows or marshmallow pops

2. The Coating
TOP WITH...

royal icing
buttercream frosting
poured sugar icing
fondant
melted candy melts

3. The Decorations
EMBELLISH WITH...

piped royal icing designs
piped buttercream frosting
fondant decorations
candy clay decorations
edible writers
paint and stamps
tinted coconut
sprinkles and candy
edible icing sheets

how to mix and match (Or what I find works best together)

Top this basic confection...	...with this coating
cookies or cookie pops	royal icing, poured sugar icing, fondant, melted candy melts
cakes and cupcakes	buttercream frosting, fondant
cake pops	melted candy melts
petits fours	fondant, poured sugar icing
marshmallows or marshmallow pops	nothing or melted candy melts

Use this coating...	...under these decorations
royal icing	piped royal icing designs, fondant and candy clay decorations, edible writers, paint and stamps, sprinkles and candy, edible icing sheets
buttercream frosting	fondant and candy clay decorations, piped buttercream frosting, tinted coconut, sprinkles and candy, edible icing sheets
poured sugar icing	piped royal icing designs, fondant and candy clay decorations, edible writers, paint and stamps, sprinkles and candy
fondant	piped royal icing designs, fondant and candy clay decorations, edible writers, paint and stamps, sprinkles and candy, edible icing sheets
melted candy melts	piped royal icing designs, piped buttercream frosting, fondant decorations, edible writers, sprinkles and candy

ACKNOWLEDGMENTS

Support of all kinds from my husband, Greg, made this book possible, as did Maeve's discerning palate and stirring and scooping skills. But Greg's and Maeve's patience during my craziness deserves the biggest mention.

Huge praise goes to those not forced to live with me. Thank you to my family, both the Mountford and Marchand sides. To my mom and my dad, for their help, presence, advice, encouragement and child care. To my sister, Catherine, for exactly the same. To my brother, Bill, for connecting me with graphic arts genius Matt LaRusso, whose advice proved invaluable. To Dale and Shirley Marchand, for their Maeve watching and ever-present willingness to help.

To my great friends, without whom I'd never have completed this book. I wish I had the pages to name you all. To the Gymboree Mammas: Liz saves me daily and takes my kid at a moment's notice, Slone is crucial to this book, as she found my photographer, and Karen delivers amazing food. To my neighbors, Kirsten and John, for listening to my book stories and occupying Maeve's attention, and to my former neighbors, Alan and Lindy, who still drop everything to get me any information I need. To Beth, for always stepping in without question to help with Maeve, and to Fresia, for the comfort in her unconditional friendship. And, of course, Sarah Kerchner, of Bundles of Cookies, deserves a big gold star for introducing me to the decorated cookie.

To my agent, Andrea Somberg, for her kindness, endurance and skills, and especially her influence in the creation of this book.

To the amazing team at Harlequin for their enthusiasm and direction. I was fortunate my introduction to Harlequin was made through the wonderful Deb Brody. And thank you to Mark Tang for your early advice.

To my brilliant photographer, Abby Greenawalt, who helped define this book visually, a feat of great magnitude, and to the eyes and mind of stylist Lisa Sikorski, who proved critical in her role.

To the owners of *Craft Gossip*, Shellie Wilson and Vikram Goyal, and to all my coeditors, for their encouragement and backing. I know what I know largely because of *Edible Crafts,* so my gratitude for this gig can't be overstated. And a thank-you to Heather Holbrook for your stamping resources advice.

To my fellow bloggers, with whom I share inspiration, jokes, gripes, camaraderie and sanity (or insanity). There are too many of you to list, but a special thank-you to Amanda Formaro, my coeditor at *Craft Gossip* and my friend, for her help with all things technical and so much more. And to Bridget of *Bake at 350,* Amanda of *i am baker,* Marian of *Sweetopia,* Cheryl of *Sew Can Do,* and Callye of *The Sweet Adventures of Sugarbelle*.

And finally, a gigantic thank-you to every one of my blog readers. Your support, comments, follows, questions, links and presence have influenced every page here.

INDEX

Page numbers of photographs appear in italics.

MY FAVORITE

Supplies + Ingredients

Techniques

Directions

MY FAVORITE

Supplies + Ingredients

Techniques

Directions

MY FAVORITE

Supplies + Ingredients

Techniques

Directions

MY FAVORITE

Supplies + Ingredients

Techniques

Directions

MY FAVORITE

Supplies + Ingredients

Techniques

Directions

MY FAVORITE

Supplies + Ingredients

Techniques

Directions